# Finding Refuge

## Real-Life Immigration Stories from Young People

### Victorya Rouse

ZEST BOOKS
MINNEAPOLIS

*To my parents*

Zest Books™
An imprint of Lerner Publishing Group, Inc.
241 First Avenue North
Minneapolis, MN 55401 USA

For reading levels and more information, look up this title at www.lernerbooks.com.
Visit us at zestbooks.net.

Image credits: Maps by Laura K. Westlund/Independent Picture Service; Irina Bg/Shutterstock.com, (profile) p. 1; The Color Archives/Alamy Stock Photo, p. 81; Nou Vang, pp. 88–97; REUTERS/Osman Orsal/Alamy Stock Photo, p. 131; arifoto UG/Michael Reichel/dpa-Zentralbild/dpa picture alliance/Alamy Stock Photo, p. 144; Rido/Shutterstock.com, p. 151; Not home/Wikimedia Commons (public domain), p. 187; REUTERS/Luc Gnago/Alamy Stock Photo, p. 196; SDI Productions/E+/Getty Images, p. 236; Ken Hawkins/Alamy Stock Photo, p. 249. Design elements: TonelloPhotography/Shutterstock.com (background); Giraffarte/Shutterstock.com (handwritten letters).

Cover profiles: Irina Bg/Shutterstock.com; ABO PHOTOGRAPHY/Shutterstock.com; michaelheim/Shutterstock.com; VALUA STUDIO/Shutterstock.com; Ollyy/Shutterstock.com. Design elements: TonelloPhotography/Shutterstock.com (background); Giraffarte/Shutterstock.com (handwritten letters).

Design by Viet Chu.
Main body text set in Janson Text LT Std. Typeface provided by Linotype AG.

**Library of Congress Cataloging-in-Publication Data**

Names: Rouse, Victorya, author.
Title: Finding refuge : real-life immigration stories from young people / Victorya Rouse.
Description: Minneapolis : Zest Books, [2021] | Includes bibliographical references and index. | Audience: Ages 11–18 | Audience: Grades 7–9 | Summary: "What is a refugee? English teacher Victorya Rouse assembles a collection of true teen immigration stories essential for our times, complete with maps, context, and background on the refugees' home countries" —Provided by publisher.
Identifiers: LCCN 2020038230 (print) | LCCN 2020038231 (ebook) | ISBN 9781541581562 (library binding) | ISBN 9781541581609 (paperback) | ISBN 9781728401645 (ebook)
Subjects: LCSH: Teenage immigrants—Juvenile literature. | Teenage refugees—Juvenile literature.
Classification: LCC HV4005 .R68 2021 (print) | LCC HV4005 (ebook) | DDC 305.235092/6912—dc23

LC record available at https://lccn.loc.gov/2020038230
LC ebook record available at https://lccn.loc.gov/2020038231

Manufactured in the United States of America
1-47340-47966-5/18/2021

# CONTENTS

## INTRODUCTION
# Do You Ever Wonder?

W hen you read about war in your history book or hear about it in the news, do you ever wonder what happens to the families and children in the places experiencing war? History books and news reports usually focus on government leaders, not the people caught in the middle of the conflict.

In our own daily lives, we have routines: getting up in the morning, eating, going to school or work, spending time with our friends, and sleeping at night. For a child living through war, nights are filled with the sounds of gunfire and bombs. Getting food to eat and water to drink can be difficult. Grocery stores and markets may be unable to get supplies. Fields and gardens may not get planted or cared for. Sometimes there is no electricity. Leaving home to go to school or to hang out with friends can be dangerous. Knowing whom to trust is hard if one group of people decides that another group is too different to live in their community. Many families in these situations decide that they must leave their homes to stay alive. What happens to them? Some of these people become refugees.

## What Is a Refugee?

The United Nations High Commissioner for Refugees (UNHCR) defines a refugee as

> . . . *someone who has been forced to flee his or her country because of persecution, war or violence. A refugee has a well-founded fear of persecution for reasons of race, religion, nationality, political opinion or membership in a particular social group.*

We all need shelter and safety. Refuge is a safe place, so a refugee is a person looking for safety.

Throughout history, people have been forced to leave their homes because of war, natural disasters, and other problems that made their homes unsafe. Usually refugees have very little time to plan their journey. Their situation changes quickly, they are in sudden danger, and they leave their homes with whatever they can carry. Sometimes families travel for days, weeks, or months, looking for refuge. When they arrive in a new place, the people who live there may not have enough food and shelter available to help them. Sometimes they are welcomed, but sometimes they are told they cannot stay and must keep going.

## Why Do People Become Refugees?

Sometimes people look at war and violence in another country and wonder, *Why do people commit such terrible acts against their own people?* Those who are persecuting others do not consider their victims to be "their own people"; they view their victims as different and dangerous. When one group of people decides that another group of people is too "different" to be tolerated, they often turn to violence to make those people go away. The victims of persecution must make the choice to leave or suffer violence, discrimination, and possibly death.

When refugees decide they must flee their homes, their destination is determined by several factors. Some are practical, such as where they are allowed to settle, where they can afford to settle, and where they can physically travel. Many countries do not allow refugees to permanently settle within their borders. Transportation to a safe place can be difficult to find and expensive. It is often dangerous. Every year hundreds of people die trying to find refuge. Other factors are emotional; refugees may have relatives or friends already living in a certain country, or they may have heard that a certain country is more accepting of their culture or beliefs than their homeland.

Often, refugees do not have a choice, and they are assigned the place where they will be resettled. Countries that receive refugees decide who and how many people they will admit. There is no perfectly safe or welcoming country where every refugee has a positive experience, but refugees make the best of the situations they find in their new homes.

## What Happens When People Become Refugees?

When people leave home looking for safety, they are asylum seekers. According to international law and the Universal Declaration of Human Rights, everyone has the right to seek asylum. People may cross borders and request asylum from the country they arrive in, or they may register with an organization to get help resettling in another country.

Before they are granted refugee status, asylum seekers must pass background checks and health checks, in addition to answering many questions to prove that they are who they say they are. People who have committed crimes are not eligible for refugee status. If their request is processed and approved, they are officially refugees, meaning they have a clear legal status in their new countries.

Sometimes, people cannot find a safe place to wait during the long and difficult application process, or they fear their application will be denied on a technicality. They may try to enter a new country without legal documentation. If discovered by authorities, they may be held in a detention facility or deported—sent to another country, often the very country they fled.

For most of history, no organizations existed to help refugees find homes and food. In 1950 the office of the UNHCR was created to help the millions of Europeans who were displaced—made homeless—by World War II (1939–1945). The UNHCR, along with other organizations, continues to help people who need to find refuge. According to the UNCHR, 70.8 million people around the world have been forced to leave their homes because of war or persecution as of 2019. Over 50 percent of these people are under the age of eighteen.

Although most refugees would like to be able to go home and resume the lives they left behind, most can never return. Sometimes they stay in refugee camps for many years before being resettled in a new country. For instance, thousands of people fleeing violence in Sudan have lived in UNHCR-run camps along the Sudanese border in neighboring countries for many years. Some people live their whole lives in refugee camps.

## Refugees in the United States

Before they leave a refugee camp, refugees resettling in the United States must agree to repay the United States government for their travel and resettlment costs. Most countries have similar requirements.

When refugees come to the United States, nonprofit organizations can help them find homes, enroll their children in schools, apply for work permits, and find jobs. Like all people working in the United States, refugees who work pay taxes.

When refugees have lived in the United States for five years, they can apply for citizenship, which involves paying an application fee, demonstrating an ability to speak and understand the English language, and taking a citizenship test. In 2020 the application fee was raised from $725.00 to $1,170.00, but the US District Court for the Northern District of California issued a nationwide preliminary injunction to stop the increase. The citizenship test has questions about the US government and history. If they pass this test, and if they have not broken any US laws, they can become citizens. New citizens swear to support and defend the Constitution of the United States and to follow the laws of the United States.

## Stories from Students

I teach high school students who are learning English for the first time. Many of the young people who come to my classroom have left countries where conflict made it impossible to live safely. They come to the United States—specifically to the city of Spokane, Washington—to escape the dangers in their countries and to begin new lives.

Starting over in a new place is not easy. Learning English is not easy with its strange spellings and irregular verbs. In my class, students practice writing in English by composing stories and essays. Frequently, they write about their lives and experiences, their struggles, and their dreams. Sometimes they write about their countries, how they came to the United States, and what their first days in the United States were like. We call these their "coming to America" stories.

The essays in this book are only some of the stories students have shared with me over the years. With the help of families, friends, and social media, I've been able to locate many of my former students to interview them about what they are doing now and to let them update their stories.

Some students had lost their original stories but were willing to sit down and retell their story for this book. Most importantly, my students told me about their lives since high school and shared what they would like people to understand about their experiences.

The students' words and sentiments are their own. They are a small sample size drawn from one community, not representatives of all immigrants or all refugees in the United States. But the experiences that brought them here—to Spokane, Washington, to my classroom—reflect the ongoing realities faced by refugees around the world.

# PART 1

# AFRICA

The name Africa comes from the Greek Aphrika, meaning "without cold." Except for mountaintops, the African continent is rarely cold.

**AREA:** 11.72 million square miles (30.35 million sq. km), second-largest continent

**POPULATION:** 1.3 billion (second most populous continent)

**COUNTRIES:** 54 countries and one "non-self-governing territory"

**LANGUAGES:** more than 1,500 languages

**RELIGIONS:** Islam, Christianity, Judaism, and traditional religions

Libya

**AFRICA**

INDIAN
OCEAN

## CHAPTER 1

# LIBYA

## A Few Facts about Libya

**AREA:** 647,184 square miles (1.68 million sq. km)

**POPULATION:** 6.87 million

**LANGUAGES:** Arabic, Berber, Italian, English

**RELIGIONS:** Islam, Christianity, and others

## A Little History

At different times in history, Libya has been controlled by the ancient Phoenicians, Greeks, Romans, and Ottoman Turks, who wanted places for their trading ships to stop along the Mediterranean Sea. In 1911 Italy occupied Libya and began a long conflict with the Arab population, who opposed colonization. The British and French occupied Libya in 1943, during World War II.

The United Nations (UN) gave Libya independence in 1951.

Libya was very poor until oil was discovered. The king made deals with Western oil companies eager to develop Libya's oil resources. This improved the Libyan economy, but many Libyans worried that the king was making decisions based on what Europeans and Americans wanted instead of what was good for Libyan people.

In 1969 a group of military officers led by Colonel Muammar al-Gaddafi took over the government, abolished the monarchy, and took control of the oil industry and other businesses in Libya. In the beginning, Gaddafi's government made many improvements in Libya in education and health care. The government built a water system that provided water to all parts of the country.

But Gaddafi also became a dictator. Libyans did not have the right to vote. They did not have freedom of speech. People who disagreed with the government were arrested, tortured, and sometimes killed. Books that Gaddafi did not agree with were burned.

The government was overthrown in December 2010, and a pro-democracy movement called the Arab Spring spread across North Africa and the Middle East. In 2011 rebels took over the Libyan government, and Gaddafi was eventually captured and killed. The new government held elections, but Libya remained in chaos as different groups continued to fight for control of the government.

## Why Did People Leave?

When the rebellion started, both the government and the police force collapsed. In addition to the fighting between the military and the rebels, crime soared. Seeking safety, people left for Europe via the Mediterranean Sea or Egypt via land.

# Amir

Libya
US Entry: 2013

I am from Sudan, but I have never lived in Sudan. I was born in Libya.

Sudan is a big country in Africa, but now it is not as big as it was because it split into two countries: The Republic of Sudan and The Republic of South Sudan. South Sudan is for Christians and the north is for Muslims. Sudan is famous for growing corn and has many sheep and camels. That is all I know about my country. I have never lived in Sudan, because my family moved to Libya before I was born. Sudan had a lot of problems, so my parents decided to move. My family moved to Benghazi, Libya.

My life in Libya was good. My friends and I played soccer and swam in the Mediterranean Sea. My favorite place in the world is by the sea. By the sea I can see people swimming and see fish, and I like to swim in the saltwater. Libya is different from America. In Spokane [Washington], the summers are so hot, but in Libya the summers are not so hot; it is warm and sunny. In Spokane, the winters are so cold and snowy, but in Libya the winters are not cold. There is no snow in Libya.

My life in Libya was good, but then life started to change.

In February 2011, a revolution began in Libya. The people turned against the president. They did not want the president anymore. The people wanted to remove President Gaddafi from the country. The president did not want to leave the presidency. The people started protesting against him. They went to the armories and they destroyed the buildings where the weapons were kept and took all the weapons. All the people went to the president's city and fought him, but he did not want to go. The people wanted the government to release political prisoners, but the president would not. In my city, Benghazi, there was no government because all the government workers left their jobs and turned against the president. The fighting was very close to our house. For months, the people fought against the army. People were dying all around us, people I knew, people I grew up with. It was not safe for the people who lived in Benghazi.

Not everyone was fighting to make a better country; some people stole stuff from people. They stole cars, people's money, and the technology and tools to make money. They were shooting people to take their money. Life in our city was not safe. People started to move out of Libya. Some moved to the east side of the country, many of them moved to Italy by boat, and some people moved to Egypt by cars. There were no airplanes to fly to the east. All my neighbors moved; some moved to Egypt and some moved to Italy. The way to Egypt was the easy way. Going to Italy was very hard and dangerous.

We were afraid for our lives. We heard there was a refugee camp in Egypt. We also heard the people at the refugee camp helped people to travel to America and Europe. My brothers did not want to go to a refugee camp. My dad said, "We will go to the refugee camp and then maybe we will travel to America."

When my dad said "America," my brothers smiled, but they were still upset. America was my dream, and my brothers dreamed to go there too. Finally, they accepted the plan to travel to the refugee camp in Egypt. In June 2011, my family prepared to go to the refugee camp.

My brother Ayad was in Tripoli [the capital city of Libya]. Tripoli was closed, so Ayad could not get out and we could not get in. My dad said, "You will have to go to Egypt. And I will wait for Ayad to come from Tripoli."

My brothers, sisters, mother, and I traveled to Egypt by a special bus for just one family. We traveled the 600 miles across Libya to Egypt. My friend's father was our driver. The weather was good. The travel was fun, like an adventure. It was my first time to see mountains—I used to live in the city where there were no mountains. We stopped and ate along the way. We had water, food like mangoes and other fruits, vegetables, milk, juice, bread, and everything we needed. We were comfortable, and happy to be leaving the dangers behind. We were thinking about how we were heading to America. It was a twelve-hour drive from Benghazi to Egypt, but we did not get tired or sick.

When we arrived in Sallum, Egypt, we saw many people that we knew from Libya. All the people that we saw were coming from Libya. I felt happy because my friends were there also.

The day after we came to Egypt from Benghazi, we went to the International Office for Migration, IOM. My mother told them what happened in Libya and what happened to our family.

We had to go to the office every day, to have interviews. In the interviews they asked us about all of our information. We finished the interview and we went back to the tent. We had many interviews.

On October 23, 2011 my dad and Ayad came to Egypt, and we were happy. Many people died in Tripoli, but my brother was safe. My dad and Ayad went to the IOM and told them why they were late. They had many interviews too.

Later the people who were responsible for us asked us to go to do blood tests. We went to the hospital and did the blood tests. After our medical check and blood tests, they said, "You guys have finished everything, so now you just have to wait to travel." That is what they said, so we felt as happy as children in the candy store. After three months, the IOM told us we would be going to the United States, but they did not tell us when. We waited almost two years in Egypt.

In the refugee camp we were just waiting and waiting. I felt so sad about my country, Libya. The people there were fighting and killing each other. People died every day. There was no safety for anyone. We wanted to go to America because it is a safe country, with no killing, no fighting, no war. In America we could get good education and jobs. We wanted to go to America because America is beautiful, and people have rights.

In 2013 we had a final interview with the jury. My mom and dad were scared because a lot of people did not pass the jury interview. After two weeks the IOM called, and they told us that we passed the interview. My family was happy, and we had a party in the house. We had our last interview, and we passed it.

A month later, we had a final medical check. We spent seven hours in the hospital. After we finished the medical check, everyone was tired.

Four months later, the IOM called my dad and they said that we were going to the United States in June 2013. We were so happy, and we could not even believe it. We started to pack up our stuff to get ready to travel. The first thing we did was sell everything in the house—the TV, furniture, everything. The second thing we did was go to the store to get new clothes and bags to put our belongings in.

On June 28, 2013 I woke up so early, and I took shower. About 6 a.m. we went to the station to ride the bus. My friends, my family, and my family's friends came with us to the station just to say goodbye. We said goodbye to each other, and some people were crying. Then we rode the bus to go to the airport in Cairo. It took six hours [to travel] from Sallum to Cairo.

During that six hours I just looked around the country, seeing how beautiful it is. My family slept. Along the way we stopped, and we ate some chicken and rice and drank juices. Finally, the bus arrived at the Cairo Airport. It was very big and nice. There were a lot of people from different countries. We spent two days in the airport and that was not nice—it was like jail. My mom was scared about the airport because the room we slept in was so bad; it was cold and crowded. Every day she went and she asked them when we were going to get out of this room.

On June 30, 2013, in the morning, we woke up and got ready to travel to the United States. My mom and dad were happy. We put all the huge luggage in the machine, and we went to the departure hall to wait for the airplane. After the airplane came, we went up to the airplane. It was my first time to get in an airplane. It was so cool in the plane. (It was not the first time for some of my family to get in a plane.) The airplane was so big and there were a lot of people on the plane. I decided I wanted to learn how to fly an airplane.

Our trip to America took twelve hours. I ate two meals and watched four movies. I was so tired. My family and I were waiting to arrive in America. When we arrived in the New York City airport I don't know how to explain the feeling that we felt, but we were too much happy.

In the airport there were so many people. I was so afraid that someone would come and talk to me because at that time I did not speak English. Just my sister could speak English. When we arrived, we met a very nice lady who was responsible for helping us to go to Spokane. She helped us a lot. She bought food for us and she drove us to the hotel. My brothers, dad, and I slept in one room, and my mom and sisters slept in a different room. I slept about six hours, but I felt like I had just closed my eyelids when someone knocked on the door. The lady came back to us and she said, "Get ready because at nine o'clock you will travel to Spokane, Washington." We got ready, and she drove us back to the airport. To travel to Washington, she told us first the plane would go to Colorado. We put our bags in the plane and then we rode the plane. About six hours later we arrived in Colorado. Our bags stayed in the plane, but we got off the plane for about one hour. Then we rode the plane again to Spokane, Washington.

When we arrived in Spokane, I saw people that we knew. Some of my friends were there too. I felt so happy because I had missed them. We hugged each other. I felt really happy because I had been traveling for so long and finally, I was in America.

Spokane was very nice and very hot. People from World Relief [a nonprofit humanitarian organization] took us to someone's house, and we spent the next four days there. Then they took us to our new house on the south hill of Spokane, and it was so nice. Our home in Spokane is so different from our home in Libya. In Spokane we have a big yard, and only two people sleep in each bedroom. In Libya we did not have a yard, and three or four people slept in each bedroom. In Spokane we have a big kitchen. Our home is beautiful, and I like our neighbors because they are so good. They are friendly and they help us if we need help.

Moving from Libya to America was difficult because Americans speak a different language, and I did not know any English. I was so confused because I did not know the language and I did not know what American people were like. I wondered, when I go to school what should I do? I thought the teachers and students would think I was stupid because I did not speak English. When I went to school, I was worried that the teachers would ask me difficult questions and I would not know how to answer because of English.

When I left my country, I left my friends and everything that I knew. It was so difficult for me. Then I went to school. The teachers taught me English, they helped me to learn everything I needed to learn. I made new friends.

Before I came to America, I thought life in America was going to be so easy, but it is not easy. We must work hard, but it is better here than life in my country. I made new friends and new life and also, I am in a safe country. I love my life in America.

# Epilogue

In high school my English teacher told me I should join the cross-country team. I did not really want to join the cross-country team, I just wanted to play soccer, but I decided to try it for a few days to make my teacher happy. When I joined the cross-country team, I made a lot of good friends and won a lot of races. I got a 4-year running scholarship to go to university. I still wanted to become a pilot, but people told me that after the 9-11 attack on the United States, no one would hire a Muslim to fly a plane. Like many people, I have changed my major a couple of times. I am studying business and will graduate from university in 2021. In 2018, I became a US citizen. In the future, I want to have a good job and help other people the way people have helped me.

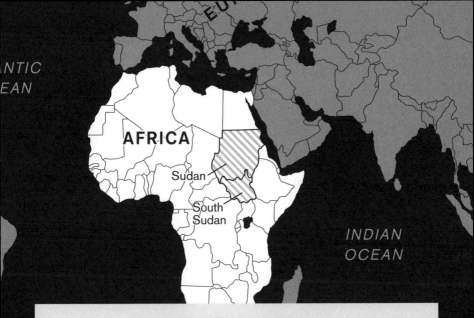

CHAPTER 2

# SUDAN

········································································

## A Few Facts about the Republic of the Sudan

**AREA:** 712,280 square miles (1.84 million sq. km)

**POPULATION:** 42.81 million

**LANGUAGES:** Arabic, English, Nubian, and Nilotic

**RELIGIONS:** Islam


## A Few Facts about the Republic of South Sudan

**AREA:** 248,777 square miles (644,329 sq. km)

**POPULATION:** 11.06 million

**LANGUAGES:** English, Swahili, and Indigenous languages

**RELIGIONS:** Christianity, Animism, and Islam

# A Little History

The Republic of the Sudan is one of the largest countries in Africa. The majority of the people in northern Sudan are Arabic-speaking Muslims, while most people in the south are ethnic African groups practicing Christianity and Animism. Despite these regional differences in religion, language, and customs, the Europeans who colonized this part of Africa in the nineteenth century made Sudan one country.

In the 1980s, northeastern Africa experienced drought. There was not enough rain to grow crops or grass for livestock. People fought over the limited resources, farmland, and grazing land. Conflict erupted between Arab Muslim northerners and Christian and animist ethnic African southerners.

In 1989 the government of Sudan was negotiating peace between the north and south when Lieutenant General Omar Ahmad al-Bashir seized power. Bashir, a member of a nomadic Arab tribe from north-central Sudan, armed Arab militia groups called the Janjaweed against their traditional African rivals. Bashir's government prevented humanitarian relief agencies from providing aid, and thousands died from the violence and famine. Caught between the Janjaweed militia and drought, ethnic Africans fled, looking for refuge in Ethiopia and Kenya.

Civil war broke out between farmers and nomads again in 2003. President Bashir began to take land away from farmers and give it to the Janjaweed militias. In addition to forcing people off their land, these militias robbed and killed thousands. Millions fled, ending up in refugee camps. The UN's International Criminal Court (ICC) charged President Bashir with war crimes and crimes against humanity in 2009 and 2010, but he ignored the ICC's arrest warrants.

In July 2011 the Republic of South Sudan split from the Republic of the Sudan and became an independent country.

The Republic of South Sudan continues to suffer ethnic violence as different tribes fight for control of the government. In 2019 Bashir was overthrown as the president of the Republic of the Sudan. The struggle for control of the government of Sudan continues.

## Why Do People Leave?

People leave Sudan to escape the ongoing violence and political instability. They seek safety, access to education, and basic human rights.

# Abdulrazik

**Sudan**
**US Entry: 2013**

My family are Masalit people from the Darfur region of Sudan, but I was born in Gedaref, in eastern Sudan, where my mother's family lived.

We were farmers, living a peaceful, traditional life of raising crops, cows, and goats. We had traditional huts made of mud and rock with thatched roofs, and a fence around the homestead. During the rainy season we would plant and cultivate crops and harvest them during the dry season. We raised enough to feed the family and if there was extra, we would sell that for cash to buy what we needed.

We lived a continuous cycle of life, without much thought or worry about the future. We had a simple life—a simple, peaceful lifestyle. The government discouraged education, advising parents that education would corrupt their children and lead them astray. My father did not agree with this. He thought education was necessary. He did not read or write, but he wanted his children to be educated. He wanted to educate his children so they could do better for the country.

Our simple life ended with the beginning of the Sudanese Civil War in 2003 when I was nine years old. This conflict was not religious, it was ethnic: ethnic African farmers versus Arab nomads. The Arab nomads did not grow crops. They kept livestock and migrated through the country. Traditionally there were small disputes between the nomads and the farmers that were settled by village elders. Everything changed when the government of Sudan under President Omar al-Bashir began to take land away from the African farmers and give it to the Arab nomads. The government bombed the African communities from the air, then the nomads called the Janjaweed would come on the ground killing people and burning everything.

My grandfather was killed in the early stages of the conflict, and my father saw that the fighting would get worse. He knew that we needed to find a new place to live. He said to my family, "We must go."

I was in Gedaref, with my mother's family, so my father came to get me. We walked through the night and day to join the rest of the family. A small lorry [truck] was there to help us get to a safer place. We were joined by other families along the way. The route my father chose was dangerous, and forbidden, but we needed to go, to find safety. We crossed through mountains and forests. Sometimes we walked and sometimes we rode in trucks with the baggage. At night we had to share one mosquito net between eight people. Sometimes the lorry got stuck in the mud, so the fathers would push. The journey was very slow.

First, we came to a camp for internally displaced people. We lived in a tent there for two years, always worried that the government would come and bomb our camp. The government was worried that the people in the camps would turn against the government. The International Rescue Committee helped with tents and basic needs.

In 2006 we were resettled into another camp inside Sudan. After two more years living in that camp, we left Sudan. We flew in a cargo plane. We could see that sometimes that plane was used to carry livestock. It was not very clean. There were no seats or seat belts. For us the cargo plane was a luxury, though, because we did not have to walk.

In 2008 we arrived in Kakuma Refugee Camp in Kenya. Again, we were living in tents. Some people in the camp had been there for fifteen or twenty years. Still, we were always hoping for two things: peace in our home country so we could return, or resettlement in a safe country so we could get education to help ourselves and others. If we could not return home, we thought, "Someday we will go to America."

We registered with the UNHCR and hoped that we could pass the screening and interview process. The interview process was very stressful. The questions were asked again and again, and the answers must be consistent. Everyone in the family must answer the same. Any differences in the answers and the family fails. Then they must stay in the camp with no hope.

Once a month we would get food rations. There were no jobs. We were not allowed to work, or to leave the camp. Every day we went to school, but we learned nothing. The schools were not very good. My father wanted us to be educated, so he left the camp and worked for a few months and came back with money for me to go to a boarding school in Kenya.

I attended the boarding school for two years, from grades 4 to 6. The school was in the Turkana region of Kenya. Twice a day we were given a 20-ounce cornmeal drink called ugli. Once a month we had meat. They would stew one goat and share it between all the students. We would each get a small portion of meat and a small scoop of rice. At this school I began to learn English and Swahili, reading and writing, math and science, history and geography. I was happy to finally be able to learn.

In 2012 my family was approved to go to the United States. We had our medical checks. In orientation we learned about school, and riding buses. We watched videos of simple everyday tasks like paying the bus fare with coins. We could not really take in this information; it did not seem real. Our minds were thinking, "When am I going to be there?"

On the last day in Kakuma, everyone cried. We said good-bye to our friends. Everyone wanted to help us carry our bags to the bus that took us out of the camp. We had waited so long. Many were still waiting.

I was eighteen. I had been a refugee for half my life.

In July 2012, we arrived in Spokane, Washington. The weather was hot, like Kenya. Everything was beautiful and different. The streets were so different, with beautiful homes and gardens. The stores were huge. The differences were overwhelming.

In Spokane we had a day of orientation with World Relief. They found us a home. Our new neighbor, Crystal, was so nice. She helped us with so many things; she showed us how to live in America, how to use the stove and ride the bus and shop. We were so lucky to have such a good neighbor. We are still friends.

All the children in my family were registered for school, but World Relief said I was too old to go to high school. I would have to get a job and learn English at the adult education center. I was so discouraged. I wanted so badly to go to school. Everyone at the adult education center was so old.

On the first day of school in September, I escorted my sister to high school. The teacher said, "Welcome to Ferris! We have been waiting for you," and told me to sit down. I was on her list. I was so happy, but I expected they would say they had made a mistake and make me leave.

They gave me a test to see how much English I knew and gave me a full schedule of classes. I went to school every day expecting to get kicked out for being too old. But I worked extra hard to learn everything I could before that happened. I came in early and stayed late every day to get extra help.

At first, I was very shy. I worried that people would laugh at me for not speaking good English. In addition to my classroom classes, I took online classes called ZERO-HOUR I-CAN to earn the credits I needed to graduate from high school. The online virtual learning classes were self-paced, and I finished them early. Every day, I was encouraged by my teachers. They believed in me. Then slowly I could see it too. I started to have more confidence in my English.

Along with some other ELD [English language development] students, I joined the soccer team. I made friends. I started to feel like I fit in. My life was good.

## Epilogue

I graduated from Ferris High School in 2015 and went to Whitworth University for one year. Then I transferred to Eastern Washington University to finish my degree in international affairs and communication. I was accepted in the Eastern Washington McNair Scholars program. I am preparing to go to graduate school to pursue a PhD in global conflict resolution. I am interested in civil conflicts that violate international laws such as human rights violation, war crimes, and genocide. My hope is to contribute in research, understanding, and resolution to conflicts that displace many people around the world. I hope to work in international organizations, especially United Nations, in peacekeeping missions.

To me, it feels like it is just the beginning as I take to the next step to graduate school to pursue my PhD.

# Michael Michelle

**South Sudan**
**US Entry: 2012**

My mother is a strong woman. I can say she is a warrior woman. She is from Sudan. She grew up in war and lost everything. Her parents were killed, and her husband was killed, but she saved her children. She saved me.

My mother found safety in Kakuma Refugee Camp, and that is where I was born.

Kakuma had people with different languages and different cultures. I am Dinka, but my friends spoke different languages, so sometimes we mixed our languages and communicated okay.

School was a dangerous place in Kakuma. The classes were very, very, big. There were maybe fifty children with one teacher. I only went to school one time, but I got beat up, so I never went back.

Once when I was about nine, some Kenyan people tried to kidnap me, but I screamed, "Help me!" in my language, and a Dinka man rescued me. Many bad things happened in Kakuma, but I do not like to think about that. I learned not to trust people too much in Kakuma.

Life in Kakuma Refugee Camp was not easy. Kakuma Refugee Camp is nothing like America. In Kakuma, food was delivered once a month: beans and rice. We had to go to the forest to gather wood to build a fire to cook. We cooked in a big iron pot over the fire. Sometimes we could gather green plants to cook with our rice and beans. We ate once a day. When my

English teacher in America told me that Americans eat three meals each day, I laughed. I thought she was joking!

In the camp we thought America was amazing. People talked about America all the time. They said America was wonderful and safe. In America everyone had opportunities. We only knew what we saw in pictures. Sometimes, maybe once a year, some Americans would bring a generator and a big screen and show a movie, like for Easter we would see a movie about Easter. We thought all the people in America were white.

My mother did the paperwork with the UNHCR to be resettled in another country. My mother and older sister went to interviews and orientations. They learned about what to expect in America, but they did not tell me or my brothers what to expect. We had no idea what it would be like to travel to America.

When the time came to leave, I was scared. Leaving everything behind was scary. I was leaving my friends and the only home I had ever known, but I had to leave. I had to learn to live my life without my friends. I gave all my clothes and everything I had to my friends and to homeless people. In America I would get new clothes, American clothes. It felt good to be able to give something to someone else.

We said goodbye, and then we went by car to a little plane that took us to a bigger plane that took us to a big city in Kenya. We stayed there for a long time, maybe a month. Then we took a very big plane to Europe, and then to Arizona, and then to Spokane, Washington.

Every place we stopped was so different, and so confusing. I was airsick on the plane. The food was so strange, I could not eat it. There were bright lights everywhere, and so many people talking and I could not understand anyone. I was feeling so sick from the airplane, I was out of it.

In Arizona, we stopped for a little while. The stores were so amazing. Everyone was saying "Welcome to America!" and they tried to give us food, but we didn't recognize this food, pizza. Finally, a Kenyan man said, "What do you want to eat?" He brought us bananas and mangoes, food we could recognize. It tasted so good. We were so hungry.

Our final stop was Spokane, Washington. It was July, and we celebrated my thirteenth birthday. In Kakuma we never celebrated birthdays, but we celebrated my birthday for the first time in Spokane. Spokane was beautiful, and people were very nice to us.

We moved into a house, and a volunteer helped us find our way around. She took us to parks and taught us basketball. She took us on picnics, and shopping. We had to learn how to use the electric stove. We never had a stove before, so she showed us how to cook on an electric stove. Before she taught us to use the stove we could not eat, we did not know how to cook the food.

Every day, I asked, "When I can I go to school?" "When will school start?" I wanted to learn so much, I couldn't wait for school to start. I wanted to make friends and learn to read. Nothing in the world meant as much to me as learning.

Finally, it was September, and school started. I was a freshman in high school, and finally, I began to learn how to read and write.

## Epilogue

In America I have learned a lot. I have finally learned to read and write.

I have learned that no matter where I go, there are good people and bad people. Many bad things have happened to me in my life, and I have a hard time trusting people. There are people who will help and people who don't. I know that I want to be the person who helps.

In 2018, I became a US citizen and changed my name to Michael Michelle. I work as a home healthcare worker and as a model.

Life is still not easy, but I dream of helping to make the world a better place, of finding a way to be a voice for people who have no opportunities, because America gave me opportunities and I want to give back.

# Elizabeth

**Dinka/Sudan**
**US Entry: 2015**

Long ago, when I was small, we lived in Sudan. I remember we lived in a small village, near a lake. Sometimes, my father would take me down to the lake and I would swim in the cool water while he washed my clothes. We would lay my clothes on a rock to dry while I played.

One day he washed my clothes and shoes and put them on the rock and while he was watching me swim, someone stole my shoes! When I came out of the water, I asked, "Where are my shoes?"

"I don't know," he answered. "Maybe someone has taken them?"

I cried all the way back to our house, until my father said, "Do not cry, I will get you a new pair of shoes."

My worries were so small and simple then, so easy to fix.

Life was good for me in the village. I lived with my parents, and my grandmother, and my twin baby brothers. I had nothing to do but play with my friends and help my mother. When the weather was too hot, my friends and I could go to the lake to swim. We had fields to grow food, a little flock of chickens, a dog, and my little donkey, Moses.

Early one summer, as the farmers were burning the fields to prepare for planting, everything changed. In the night Janjaweed rebels attacked the village, burned some houses, and left. Everyone knew they would be back. The community gathered to decide what to do. People argued. We were all afraid. I was afraid.

Finally, my parents decided we would leave the village that night. We heard that there was an army commander in the forest, who was traveling to Ethiopia, taking children whose parents had died. People went to him and asked him if they could follow him to Ethiopia.

That afternoon I went to bed early, to rest before we started our journey. In my sleep, I heard my father tell my mother that it was time to get me. In the warm night, I held my grandmother one last time. She was so old. She could not run. She could not come with us. I thought of my grandmother, my friends, my little chickens, everything I was leaving behind. I was so scared. Where would we go? Where would we hide? Would we be safe? I cried as I followed my mother out of our home. My parents had packed all our things, everything we could carry with the help of my Moses. My mother carried my baby brothers in a basket balanced on her head. My father held my hand and led my donkey. Our dog followed along behind.

We left, into the forest. We had to find our way, there was no road to follow. For miles and miles, hours and hours, we walked through the bush, hoping we were going the right way. I was tired, and hungry, and thirsty. There was no resting, no sleeping, just walking. Sometimes I rode Moses for a little while to rest my little feet.

No one wanted to walk with us because of the babies. Twins are considered bad luck by some people, and people were afraid that the twins would cry, and the rebels would hear them, and attack us all. We followed behind the group.

Whenever we found a place to stop and rest, and eat, and drink, I was so happy. To see my mother cooking a meal, and sitting together, was almost like home. I had no friends to play with, so I played with our dog and Moses. The twins were too tiny to play. We could not stay in one place for long though, the rebels would find us. If the Janjaweed rebels found us, they would kill us. So, we kept traveling, following the other people.

As days and miles passed, my father's friend grew sick. There was no doctor to help him, no medicine for him to take. The journey was hard, walking and walking, miles and miles, with no rest, not enough food, not enough water. He was too sick. As he walked, he grew weaker. He passed away on the path. His family had to go on without him.

By the time we reached the middle of our country, the food my mother had packed was gone. We had eaten so little each day, but still, it was gone. My mother started to sell or trade the things we had brought with us. She sold everything to buy food from the homes we passed, until all my things, my clothes and my shoes, were gone. Now I rode my little Moses to save my feet. He was so thin, but we had nothing else for him to carry. I hugged his thin neck and thought about my grandmother, my little chickens.

We walked for two months. Our dog disappeared one night. When we reached Kurmuk, in eastern Sudan, we were all very thin. My little Moses laid down, too tired and too thin to go on. I cried and begged him to get up, but he died. Now we had nothing left.

In Kurmuk, people were coming from many different places. There were so many people. People saw my mother had twin babies and said she must ride in the big truck that was taking people to Ethiopia. The truck was very crowded, but we did not have to walk.

When we reached Ethiopia, people from the UN came. They interviewed us and all the families coming from Sudan into Ethiopia. They helped us with food and shelter.

Then we started a new life [at] Sherkole Refugee Camp. We lived in a tent until a family that had built a house, let us share with them. It was not an easy life, because there were many people coming, and the UN could not help all the people at the same time. But it was a little bit easier life, a little bit safer life. The refugee camp became the place we lived, the place we grew up, my brothers and me.

When my brothers were old enough to start to walk, we realized that one of the twins, my brother Ngor, had a disability. He could not walk. A woman from the United Nations helped us to look for help for Ngor. We made many trips to Addis Ababa to hospitals and doctors. The doctors said, "Ngor has cerebral palsy. You must go to the USA." But we did not get our papers to go to the USA for many years.

Two more brothers and a sister were born in Sherkole Refugee Camp. Every time a new child was born, we had to start our paperwork again.

I met my first love in Sherkole and had a beautiful baby girl that my brother Ngor named "Addis". We lived our lives waiting and waiting. We had many interviews and many medical checks. Finally, after 16 years of waiting, we were given papers to come to the United States. We took the bus to Addis Ababa one last time. During the night my backpack was stolen from the top of the bus. All my clothes, all my documents, were stolen. I only had the clothes I was wearing!

We had to stay at a compound while we waited for our flight to America. I begged for a chance to go out to buy some clothes, but they said, "No." Finally, someone helped me get some clothes.

We were so excited to have tickets to America. It was a beautiful feeling. We traveled for 3 days, changing planes, waiting in airports, in so many places. We were so tired. The little ones would fall asleep wherever we stopped.

Finally, we arrived in Spokane, Washington. The time difference made it hard to stay awake in the day time and to sleep at night. World Relief helped us move into a house near our new schools.

I was 18, all grown up, but I had to start over like a little child, learning a new language, learning how to live in America, in a home with electricity and running water. It was not easy, sometimes I cried, but I learned. I learned how to read English, how to ride a bus, then how to drive a car. I learned math and science, and history. I began a new life.

## Epilogue

I graduated from Spokane Community College in 2019. Now I am getting ready to study for my bachelor's degree. I have a job as a home health care aid. I love my work, but it is not easy to work and study and raise my daughter. I have to help my parents too. Sometimes I still cry and want to give up, but I keep trying. I would like to become a businessperson, but maybe I will become a social worker and help people.

I dream of giving my daughter a good life. I want her to be happy and healthy, to go to school, and to achieve her own dreams.

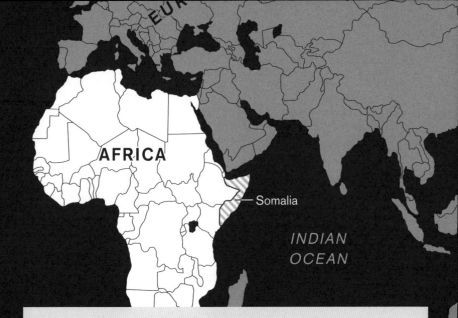

AFRICA

Somalia

INDIAN
OCEAN

## CHAPTER 3

# SOMALIA

∙∙∙∙∙∙∙∙∙∙∙∙∙∙∙∙∙∙∙∙∙∙∙∙∙∙∙∙∙∙∙∙∙∙∙∙∙∙∙∙∙∙∙∙∙∙∙∙∙∙∙∙

## A Few Facts about Somalia

**AREA:** 246,201 square miles (637,657 sq. km)

**POPULATION:** 15.44 million

**LANGUAGES:** Somali, Arabic, Italian, English, and Swahili

**RELIGIONS:** Islam

## A Little History

Like most coastal countries, Somalia has a long history of international trade. Arab and Persian traders were trading along the Somali coast as early as 600 CE. Most Somali people converted to Islam in the fourteenth century, and Islam remains the country's dominant religion. During the 1800s, Britain, France, and Italy claimed land along the Somali coast. When the Suez Canal opened in 1869, connecting the Mediterranean Sea with the Red Sea, Somalia became even more important for trade and shipping between Europe and Asia.

In 1960 Britain and Italy granted independence to their colonized territories in this region, and the Republic of Somalia was formed.

In 1969 a group of rebels led by General Mohamed Siad Barre took power. Barre's government seized control of businesses and banks. Barre also changed the Somali writing system to the Roman alphabet, which is the alphabet used for English. Barre's goal was to improve literacy and quality of life for the Somali people, but he was also authoritarian and suppressed civil rights. There were no elections, and people did not have the right to disagree with the government.

Somali society is organized into clans, or family groups. Barre's government outlawed clan loyalty, but the clan system continued to be a very strong force in the country. By 1990 the clans had organized militias, and in 1991 they overthrew Barre. Afterward, Somalia did not have a central government. The country was thrown into chaos and more fighting. In 2012 a new government was established to try to bring peace, democratic elections, unity, and stability to the country.

## Why Do People Leave?

After decades of war and political strife, people leave Somalia to find a safer place to live. They hope for educational opportunities and futures without war.

# Liban

**Somalia/Djibouti**
**US Entry: 2013**

I grew up in the Ali Addeh Refugee Camp in Djibouti, on the Horn of Africa. My parents lived there in that refugee camp for almost twenty years. My parents moved to the camp when the war started. They were young then. Most of my siblings were born in the camp. I am the fifth child in my family. I have seven brothers and three sisters. I also had two sisters and one brother who died when they were young.

My dad used to work in the city when we lived in the refugee camp. He had a job fixing watches, phones, and other electronics. When I was young my dad used to tell me that one day, I would be an engineer because I used to help him fixing things in his shop. I would get his tools ready and help him with everything he was working on. My father worked hard so he could make money for us, so my siblings and I could have an education.

The school outside the camp cost a lot of money, but it was a better school. The school in the camp was free but not very good. The school in the refugee camp taught English, but the school outside the camp in Djibouti taught French and Arabic too.

My parents worked really hard to give us the best possible life, but it was not easy. My brothers and I were not always good—sometimes we would run off and play soccer when we were supposed to be working, and sometimes we got in fights. My mother had a lot of work taking care of all of us.

In the camp, we went to school Sunday through Thursday. Friday and Saturday were our weekend. At 6 a.m. I would go to religious school to learn the Koran. Then I would come home, take a shower, and go to regular school. After school we would all play soccer. On Saturdays we would have to walk to get firewood. The firewood was a long way away, like an hour or more walking. We needed firewood for cooking.

When I was thirteen years old, my parents received a message that we had been accepted to go to America, but they kept it secret from us. They just started saving money and selling things we couldn't take with us. They knew that if they told us, even if they told us not to tell anyone, we would tell people. Sometimes people would say bad things about people who were leaving, to get them in trouble so they couldn't leave. You can't go to America if you do something bad. Also, some people might steal from you if they knew you were getting ready to leave. They would know that you had money, and they would take it.

The names of the people who were going to leave were posted on a big bulletin board a couple of weeks before they left, so finally my parents had to tell us. When I learned we were going to leave Djibouti I got really excited. We had a party to say goodbye and give away the stuff we weren't going to take with. It was strange to think I was going to leave my friends behind.

My brothers and I didn't know exactly when we were going to leave. On the day the bus came to get us, we were on our way to get firewood, and one of our brothers came running to tell us to come back—the bus was going to leave without us! I never ran so fast in all of my life! If we had missed the bus maybe I would never have come to America!

The day we left Djibouti was hot and sunny, like it always is in Djibouti, but in America it was winter. We didn't know what that even meant.

The bus took us to the city. We stayed there in a hotel for a few days, having our medical checks to make sure we were healthy enough to go to America. That was when I started to feel like I was really going to the United States.

Then it was time to leave. We took a bus to the airport and got on our first plane. It was a little scary. We flew from Djibouti to France, and then New York. In New York, we stopped overnight and slept in a hotel. New York was COLD. We were traveling with another family, and the man was bald. He stepped out of the building and his hat blew off. The snow touched his head, and he said, "Whoa! What is this?" We never knew anything could be so cold.

When we arrived in Spokane it was cold and snowy. World Relief picked us up from the airport in a van. I looked out the window, watching the snow. I wondered, "How does anyone live in snow?"

For the first two weeks we lived in a hotel.

We had such a big family that they had a hard time finding a house big enough for us. The KREM-2 News put us on the TV as the biggest refugee family. That is how we finally found a house. Someone saw us on TV and had a house for us to rent.

Once we moved into our house, we had to learn how to live in America. My brothers and I would walk around and try to learn where things were. We had our address on a piece of paper, in case we got lost. We would walk around for a while and then find our way back home. It was so cool to be in America.

It took us a while to learn how to go shopping. The boxes and cans make it hard to tell what is inside. Sometimes we didn't get what we thought we were getting. Once we had pasta with cherry sauce instead of tomatoes.

We went to the basketball court a lot, and the other kids were so nice to us. They always played with us and helped us learn English. I started school in middle school. Middle school was good; I learned so much.

People helped us so much. That summer I started playing club soccer. A family sponsored me. They picked me up and took me to practice and games. Soccer has always been my number one interest of all time. My dad used to take me to watch soccer games. My dad always supports me and believes in me, especially when it comes to soccer. I remember playing soccer barefoot on the sandy beach of the Red Sea. My friends and I played soccer every chance we could get. When I got my first pair of soccer cleats in America, I thought I would never be able to play in shoes; I had always played barefoot. But I learned. I always dream of becoming a professional soccer player. When he was young, my dad's dream was to become a professional soccer player too. He played soccer all the time too. Then everything changed—the civil war began, and not only my father's dream got destroyed, so did most of my country.

After the war began, my dad's dream was to come to the United States of America, to give us opportunity to have a better life than he had. My father's dreams motivate me now. My parents and my big brothers never graduated from high school and that also motivates me to get an education.

## Epilogue

When I was a junior in high school, my family moved to Minnesota because other Somali families kept saying, "You need to move here. Minnesota is the best place to live." A lot of Somali people live in Minnesota, but there are not many Somali people in Spokane. I did not want to move. I wanted to graduate from Ferris High School in Spokane. I stayed in Spokane with one of my brothers and his wife and worked as a dishwasher at Ferrante's Restaurant. Then my brother decided to move to Minnesota too. It was hard living on my own, so after a few months, I moved to Minnesota too.

I graduated from high school in Minnesota and started going to Minnesota Technical College. I hope to become an engineer someday, just like my dad said. I am married now, and I have a daughter, so I have to work hard. I know I can make my dreams come true if I keep working at it. I am working hard to make my family proud of me, and to make a good life for myself and my family.

# Qali

**Somalia**
**US Entry: 2016**

I was born in Mogadishu, Somalia in the year 2000. My life in Mogadishu was awesome. I had everything I needed. I had a happy family: my parents, my grandparents, and my two older brothers. My father had a business selling gold jewelry in the city, and we were happy. All of that changed in a minute, like the blink of an eye or the snap of fingers.

One sunny day when I was four years old, I was playing with my father, and suddenly he was gone. He was shot dead by a terrorist. My mother grabbed me and my brothers, and we ran. My grandparents ran with us. People were all around us crying and screaming. We were all in shock. There were gun shots and fires. Houses were burning and people were dying. There was no time to stop and pack things we needed; we just ran for our lives. This was the Somali Civil War.

My mother carried me on her back, and my brothers walked beside her. Many people were walking and running with us. Along the way, my grandparents were killed, shot by terrorists.

Some people decided to go to Ethiopia, and some decided to go to Kenya. We traveled to Kenya. People with big buses and trucks came to help the people who were leaving Somalia. The trucks were so crowded with people who were crying, so crowded we could not sit or move, we could only stand. My mother had me on her back, while she and my brothers stood.

The trucks traveled for days, stopping to let people rest under trees and go to the bathroom, then continuing. No one had food to eat, just the water the owners of the trucks had brought to share. The trucks were going and stopping, going and stopping, for three or four days.

In Kenya we stopped at Mandera for a couple of days, then we took a second bus to Nairobi. We had no money, we had nothing but our lives, so we were grateful that Kenyan people with good hearts helped us. At that time, we did not know anything about the UNHCR or how to get help from them.

We did not speak Swahili, and it was so hard to not understand anything, to not be able to communicate with people. Kind people helped us to find an apartment, and my mother got a job sewing. Sewing did not require talking to people. Later she got a second job selling tea.

Life seemed so weird. Everyone around us spoke Swahili, but no one in my family spoke Swahili. I did not understand, and I just cried all the time. My brothers and I stayed in our apartment and they tried to make me happy so I would stop crying. We were a small family. My parents had no brothers or sisters, so we had no aunties or uncles. My brothers were eight and ten years old, and they took care of me while our mother was at work.

After a while we learned to speak Swahili. My friends in Kenya also spoke English, so I learned to speak English too. My brothers did not go to school because our mother could not afford school fees. They found jobs to help support our family.

When I turned five, I started school. I loved school. At school we only spoke English, or we would get beaten. I learned reading, writing, math and science, and Swahili. I made friends. I had great teachers. Sometimes we would go on field trips to see the wild animals or the place that generates electricity. Our field trips were very interesting, but I always got carsick on the bus.

After a while I felt like I had always lived in Nairobi. If anyone asked, "Where are you from?" I would say, "I am from here. I am from Nairobi."

I went to school until fourth grade. Then my mother did not have enough money for school fees, so I had to stop going to school.

I started to help my mother to sell tea. We made big thermoses of tea, and we would carry them to shops and businesses and serve tea. In the evening we would go back to collect the cups and the money. My job was to keep track of the money. This was a good business, but it was not as good as going to school.

When I had to leave school, my mother went to the UNHCR for help. She began the process to go to another country. Many people had been waiting for twenty or thirty years to go to another country. There were so many interviews. They would ask questions, and more questions. They would ask the same questions again and again.

In 2015, they said, "Your papers are on hold." This was very stressful. "You are on hold" means you cannot go anywhere.

Then in 2016, we were told, "You are going to the United States. To Spokane, Washington."

I was so excited: "WOW!" I googled it on my cell phone and saw where Spokane, Washington was. First my brothers did not believe me. They said, "Stop fooling around." I showed them on the phone, the notice that said we were going to Washington.

My brothers asked, "Are we going to Washington, DC?"

I said, "No, Washington STATE." I showed them where it was.

We had three days of orientation. In our hearts we were already Americans. We only said goodbye to a few people we trusted. We did not tell anyone else. Sometimes when people learn that a family is going to America, they do something bad to stop them from going, so we kept it a secret. Bad things happen when people know you are leaving.

We sold everything we were not going to take with us. We gave the tea delivery business to our neighbor. Then it was time to go. We woke up early in the morning, 4 a.m. It was a cold November morning. The night before we had booked a cab to come and take us to the place where we would have our last medical checks and get our papers to go to America. We arrived there at 7:30 a.m. Then at 2:30 p.m., a bus took everyone who was leaving Kenya to Jomo Kenyatta Airport. Some people were going to England and other places; some people were going to different places in the United States.

We had to go through security. They checked everything. Then we waited. A strange man and my oldest brother were called up to the desk because "There is something in the system." The security people took them away. We were so frightened. Fifteen minutes later, my brother came back. The other man never came back.

Then it was time to get on the plane. I was so excited and happy, but I was scared too. The plane ride was very long. I got airsick. I was sick for the whole trip, and I was afraid to get up out of my seat to go to the bathroom on the plane. We flew from Nairobi to Frankfurt, Germany, and changed planes. Then we flew to Houston, Texas. We spent the night in a hotel in Houston, and they told us we were the first refugee family to stay there. They gave us tea and bread, and we slept. It was wonderful to be off the plane and sleep. The next morning, we flew from Houston to Denver, and then to Spokane.

We arrived in Spokane on a Friday night. We were met by Jackson from World Relief. He had brought an interpreter with him, to help us, but I did not need an interpreter. I told him, "We speak English." The only thing we didn't know was snow. It was so cold! I never knew anything could be so cold as snow.

That weekend we stayed in a hotel, and on Monday we went to our new apartment. In Nairobi we only had one room. Our new apartment was much bigger—it had two bedrooms. We were surrounded by a refugee community. We had friends right away. My mother found a friend from Kenya. My brothers were too old to go to school, so they went to work. They had to learn English in night school. I was sixteen. At last I could go to school again. The first day, we walked around and tried to find Ferris High School. First, we got lost, but then we found the school.

American schools and Kenyan schools are very different. In Kenya the students stay in the same classroom all day and the teachers move. In America, the teachers stay in the same classroom, and the students move. We had to leave school to eat our lunch in Kenya, but in America there is a school cafeteria. In Kenya there were not so many different classes as in America.

The first thing I had to do when I came to school was take an English test. This was not too hard for me, and I was placed in a second-level English class. I did not have any school papers from Kenya, so I was registered as a freshman. My new high school was so big and had so many classes to choose from, and no school fees. The schools in Kenya do not have school buses, either. I was amazed to see that students could take a bus to school.

In the beginning, I needed a lot of help, and the other immigrant students helped me with my classes. I made many friends, and I met other students who could speak Swahili. After a couple of weeks, I knew my schedule and I could find my way around the school.

Getting to school was very hard. I lived close enough to school to walk to school, but in the winter, there is so much snow and ice! I fell down so many times on the ice. I was happy when spring came and the snow melted away. By the time the snow melted, I felt at home in Spokane.

## Epilogue

I graduated from high school in 2020 and started college. There are so many choices! I think I will major in nursing or social work, so I can help people. Being in America has given me an opportunity to see what I am capable of doing. I can make my mother proud of who I am.

AFRICA

Eritrea

Ethiopia

*EUR...*

INDIAN
OCEAN

## CHAPTER 4

# ERITREA AND ETHIOPIA

## A Few Facts about Eritrea

**AREA:** 46,760 square miles (121,100 sq. km)

**POPULATION:** 6.08 million

**LANGUAGES:** Tigrinya, Tigré, and other Indigenous languages

**RELIGIONS:** Islam and Christianity

## A Few Facts about Ethiopia

**AREA:** 410,678 square miles (1,063,652 sq. km)

**POPULATION:** 111.93 million

**LANGUAGES:** Oromo, Amharic, Somali, Tigrinya, and other Indigenous
languages

**RELIGIONS:** Christianity, Islam, and Judaism

# A Little History

Eritrea is mostly desert. The land and climate are not good for agriculture, but many Eritrean people rely on subsistence farming to feed their families. Throughout history, Eritrea has also been an important stop on the trade routes of the Red Sea. In the 1500s, the Eritrean coast was claimed by the Ottoman Empire. Italy claimed Eritrea as an Italian colony in 1890.

During World War II, the British briefly took control and established a military communication base, Kagnew Station, in Asmara. In 1952 the United Nations made Eritrea an independent region within Ethiopia, meaning that it was technically still part of Ethiopia but had its own government. In 1953 the United States signed a treaty with Ethiopia that gave the US military control over the Kagnew military base. This base allowed US military leaders to communicate with military forces in Southeast Asia during the Vietnam War (1955–1975). The United States maintained the Kagnew military communications base until 1977.

In 1961 a group of Eritreans formed the Eritrean Liberation Front and tried to break away from Ethiopia. The civil war lasted thirty years and resulted in many people fleeing to refugee camps in Ethiopia and Sudan.

In 1993 Eritrea officially became a member of the United Nations, recognized as an independent nation. By 1998 Ethiopia and Eritrea were at war again, fighting over land that both countries claimed.

During the war, Eritrean president Isaias Afwerki canceled elections, shut down newspapers and media, and imposed military rule. The people did not have freedom of speech or religion. Anyone who disagreed with Afwerki was arrested and charged with treason. All young people were required to join the military at the age of eighteen and stay enlisted for as long as the government wanted them to serve. This unending military service caused many young Eritreans to flee to other countries.

In 2018 Eritrea signed a peace treaty with Ethiopia to end the border disputes and begin "a new era of peace and friendship." However, Eritrea laws still limit freedom of speech, the press, and religion, and young people are still forced to serve in the military.

## Why Do People Leave?

People leave Eritrea to avoid unending military service and to gain access to more civil rights, education, and opportunities.

# Luwam

**Eritrea**
**US Entry: 2016**

One afternoon, when I was nine years old, I left my country, Eritrea.

I was with my mom and with my little twin brother and sister, and then I decided to go to Ethiopia. I told my mother I was going to visit my friend, but that was a lie. I told my mom this lie because if I told her the truth, she would not have let me go to Ethiopia. It was a very dangerous journey. So I didn't have any choice—I had to tell my mom that lie. Instead of going to visit my friend, my cousin and I snuck across the border to Ethiopia. My village was only a half hour walk from the border.

That was a difficult and confusing time for me. My life was very hard in Eritrea. My family was very poor. My father had deserted my mother, and my mother had a hard time taking care of my siblings and me. She did not have anyone to help her farm and take care of the crops. Even though I was a good student and I loved school, she would make me stay home to take care of the twins. We were very poor, and sometimes we did not have enough food. Also, life in my country was difficult and dangerous. My country was fighting with Ethiopia. When young people turn eighteen, they must join the military. I didn't want to join the military. I did not want to fight in a war. My older sister had gone to Ethiopia when I was about five years old, so I decided to go to Ethiopia too. Maybe I could find my sister.

My cousin and I crossed the river into Ethiopia. Then my cousin started to cry. She said, "No, I don't want to go!"

Then I said, "Please, we have to go. If the soldiers see us, they are going to shoot us!" We had come too far to turn back.

After we crossed the border, we walked for a long way. Some children saw us and thought we were Eritrean soldiers and called out loudly. The Ethiopian authorities found us. They spoke a language we did not understand. We were afraid because we thought they were going to beat us. One lady came and brought us water, but we were so scared, we were even afraid to drink the water. They took us to a refugee camp.

They took us to an office and asked us about our families and where we were from. The interview was very hard because they asked us where the Eritrean soldiers were. They asked us political questions. We told them the truth: "We don't know."

Then they took us to a very dirty room. Children who were there before us wrote their names and villages on the wall. We stayed there for two days. Then they took us to a different refugee camp that was a long way away. Then we had a second interview. They asked the same questions for a long time.

The welcoming food was just small, thin bread and watery soup. There were so many children.

From that town they took us to another camp a long way away. We stayed in this camp for a long time. It was so nasty. My cousin and I shared one blanket, and the floor was dirty, with many insects and small snakes. Even if we were thirsty, we had to wait until mealtime to drink water. I wore the same clothes the whole time. They didn't give us any soap, only water to clean ourselves.

After a long time, they took us to another camp, Baguna, and finally we got soap and a change of clothes. Underage children like my cousin and I were kept in one house all together.

A woman would come to make food for us. We took turns carrying water. I could not miss my turn to work or I would have to do twice as much work.

In the refugee camp they fed us one piece of flat bread and one cup of tea in the morning. On the weekend we got milk. For lunch we got bread and a soup made from garbanzo bean powder watered down to make it go further.

Sometimes they asked me, "Do you want to see your mother?" When I said, "Yes," they told me I could never see her.

We went to UNHCR to apply to go to another country, to go to America. They took our pictures and put our information and pictures in the computer. I told them, "I have a sister, but I do not know what refugee camp she is in." I asked for help to find my sister.

They brought me my sister's picture. I cried when I saw her picture. They told me they would take me to my sister, but they made me wait a long time because I did not have any money. If you have money your paperwork gets done very quickly. If you do not have any money you will wait for years in the refugee camp. I did not have any money.

My cousin and I stayed together in Ethiopia for three years. Then she left to another country. She is in Holland [the Netherlands] now.

Finally, they took me to my sister. When we saw each other we cried and hugged.

Then I got malaria. My sister carried me like a baby because I could not walk. I was so cold, even though the weather was really hot. I had a high fever. My sister took me to the medical clinic and gave me medicine. She stayed with me in the clinic while I was sick.

My sister had been in the camp for five years. She already had her papers to go to Australia. She wanted to take me with her, but they said if she wanted to be with me, she would have to wait for my paperwork, and that could take many more years. My sister had seen many young children be encouraged to smoke, to do drugs, to be used for sex. She warned me not to do any bad things to harm myself. She warned me not to try to go to Sudan or back to Eritrea. She was so worried about me. She asked her friends at the camp to look after me. She cried when she left the camp. She called from Addis Ababa before she flew to Australia and cried some more. She called when she got to Australia, and we cried some more.

I stayed in Ethiopia for two more years. Life was hard without my family and I wasn't happy in Ethiopia. I was living with ten other girls in one room in the refugee camp. Sometimes we were singing, sometimes we were crying.

I did not listen to all of my sister's advice. I tried to escape to Sudan and was captured and returned many times. Many times, I tried to go back Eritrea, but they caught me at the border and took me back to Ethiopia every time, back to the camp. Many bad things happened to me at the camp. Twice I tried to kill myself, but I lived.

Finally, a friend of my sister helped me get my papers processed so I could leave the camp.

In December 2016, my papers were ready, I would go to the United States. I was fifteen years old. My sister sent money from Australia. The girls I lived with organized a big party. This was my last night in the camp.

The next morning, I said goodbye to my friends, and we cried, because I had known them for a long time, and I would miss them so much. For years we had lived together in that one room. I felt like my roommates were like my family.

The car came to pick me up. My friends helped me load my suitcase. I gave them each a hug, got in the car, and waved goodbye. The whole trip I cried and cried because I had lived there for five years, and so much had happened!

I flew on a plane to America. It took a long time, with many stops. Everything was so confusing. I cried a lot.

In America I lived with a foster family. They did not speak my language and I did not speak their language. I think I cried for three months. I started school and started to learn English and everything else students need to learn in school. I made friends. Life became easier.

## Epilogue

I lived with three different foster families. Then in 2019, I got an apartment of my own. In 2020, I graduated from high school and had a beautiful baby girl. Now I have a job working for Amazon. When my daughter is a little older, I plan to go to university. I do not know what I will study, but I want to be a useful person. I want to help people and give my daughter a beautiful life.

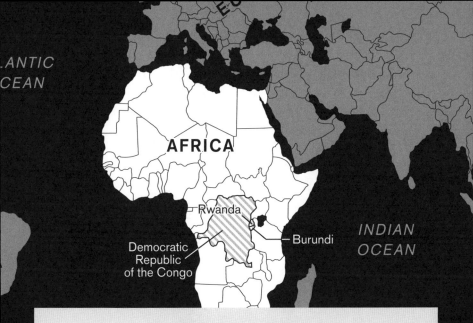

## CHAPTER 5

# CONGO, RWANDA, AND BURUNDI

## A Few Facts about the Democratic Republic of the Congo

**AREA:** 905,568 square miles (2,345,410 sq. km)

**POPULATION:** 101.8 million

**LANGUAGES:** Kiluba, Lingala, Swahili, French, and more than 200 others

**RELIGIONS:** Christianity, Islam, and traditional religions

# A Few Facts about the Republic of Rwanda

**AREA:** 10,185 square miles (26,379 sq. km)

**POPULATION:** 12.7 million

**LANGUAGES:** Kinyarwanda, Swahili, French, and English

**RELIGIONS:** Christianity, Islam, and traditional religions

# A Few Facts about Burundi

**AREA:** 10,747 square miles (27,834 sq. km)

**POPULATION:** 12.5 million

**LANGUAGES:** Kirundi, Swahili, French, and English

**RELIGIONS:** Christianity, traditional religions, and Islam

# A Little History

The Democratic Republic of the Congo and parts of Rwanda and Burundi, along with the Republic of the Congo, are located in the Congo basin, which is rich in natural resources: fertile soil, water for farming, and many valuable minerals. Europeans first reached the Congo basin in the 1480s and started to trade with Indigenous peoples for ivory and enslaved people. Europeans captured and enslaved millions of Africans in this region, sending them to Europe and the Americas.

European countries colonized land all over Africa as they looked for natural resources such as rubber, ivory, copper, gold, and diamonds. These resources made the Europeans rich, but not the Africans. People resisted European rule. In the 1960s the Democratic Republic of the Congo, Rwanda, and Burundi became independent nations.

The colonial powers had encouraged friction among different tribes, which made intertribal cooperation difficult and threw the countries into chaos. In 1965 Joseph Mobutu overthrew the government of Congo, made himself the president, and renamed the country Zaire. Mobutu took control of foreign-owned companies and used Zaire's wealth to make himself one of the richest people in the world, while the country became poorer and poorer.

In Rwanda and Burundi, the Tutsi and Hutu tribes clashed. In 1972 the Tutsis controlled the government in Burundi and committed genocide against the Hutus. Thousands of Hutus fled to Rwanda, Zaire, and Tanzania. In 1994 the Hutu presidents of Burundi and Rwanda were killed in a plane crash. The Hutus blamed the Tutsis and began to kill Tutsis. Thousands fled to refugee camps in Zaire. About eight hundred thousand people—Tutsis and Hutus who tried to protect Tutsis—were killed in what became known as the Rwandan genocide.

In 1996 Tutsi rebels overthrew Mobutu and renamed Zaire the Democratic Republic of the Congo. In spite of signing a peace agreement in 1999, fighting between Hutus, Tutsis, and Congolese continued throughout the early 2000s. The ICC charged many leaders with crimes against humanity. In 2013 a peace accord was signed to end the violence, but the DRC, Rwanda, and Burundi have not yet been able to overcome their past and maintain peace.

## Why Did People Leave?

People left to escape genocide. Even after the violence subsided, returning home after years in refugee camps was not always possible or safe. Many people were born in the refugee camps and had no homes to return to.

# Erike

**Congo**
**US Entry: 2007**

My family is from Burundi, but I was born in Congo. There in Congo, it is not easy to live. If you do not work, you do not eat. When I was a boy, my older brother and I would go to the river and get fish and sell the fish at the market. That way we would get money to buy clothes and food, the things we needed to live. I was not able to go to school because my parents did not have money to pay the school fees for me to go to school. I had to work to get money for the family.

We moved from Congo to Kigoma, Tanzania in maybe 1996 because of the war.

What I remember is that there were Hutu and Tutsi; the Tutsi and the Hutu did not like each other. The Tutsi came into a house looking for Hutus and asked, "Are you Hutu or Tutsi?" If you were Hutu, they killed you. The Hutu came into a house looking for Tutsi and asked, "Are you Hutu or Tutsi?" If you were Tutsi, they killed you. The soldiers were very cruel. I saw them take a baby and throw it into the air, and then catch that baby on a long knife, and just kill it. What kind of people would kill a baby? Sometimes the soldiers would take boys and force them to become soldiers.

In Congo, life was dangerous. Everyone needed to be ready to run at any time, like the animals must be ready to run if the lion comes. One day, my family was outside and saw that the Tutsi soldiers were coming. My parents had to run; they were hiding in the jungle. But I was in the house. I did not see the soldiers coming, so I did not run with them.

The soldiers came into my house, where I was alone. They asked, "Are you Hutu or Tutsi?" I did not say anything. The soldier put a gun in my mouth and said, "If you don't answer I will shoot you." I did not say anything.

The boss soldier said, "Just leave him." God protected me that day.

My mother came back for me, but sometimes the soldiers would leave but not really leave. Then they would come back to get people who came out of the jungle. They saw my mother go into the house, and they turned around to come back. She got me into the jungle and went back to get a blanket and the other things we needed. She jumped out of the window and the soldiers did not find her. When she was running, my mother tripped and caught her foot in a broken drainage pipe. She was stuck there with her leg trapped for a long time, maybe three days. She had to be quiet so the soldiers did not find her. God protected her, and the soldiers did not find her. Then my older brother went to get her. Her leg was hurt very badly. A doctor gave her medicine, and after a while her leg was better. We decided we had to leave Congo then.

We took a boat across Lake Tanganyika; it took two days with no food and no drink to cross that lake. Many people were on the boat. People were hungry and crying. Some people died. Thanks to God, my family lived.

We stayed in Kigoma for a couple of years. Then we had to move. The UNHCR moved us to a refugee camp. We lived in different camps: first Karago, then Mtendeli, and then Nduta. I started school in Mtendeli in second grade.

We stayed in Nduta a couple of months, then went back to Mtendeli. We wanted to find a good place to live. The people who lived in the camps did not like new people. They didn't hurt us, but they didn't help us. They didn't answer our questions if we needed help. They said, "Go back where you came from." So we went back to Mtendeli.

I went to school there in Mtendeli until sixth grade. In our school we needed to have uniforms and shoes to go to school. If we didn't have uniforms, we could not go to school. We had to buy a uniform and shoes. School in Mtendeli did not serve lunch. We had to go home for lunch or go hungry. If the teacher asked a student a question and the student did not answer, the teacher would beat the student. Every day the teacher would ask me questions, and then beat me if I did not know the answers. At the end of the sixth grade, we had a big test to see if we could go on. If we did not pass, we could not go to school anymore. The teachers told me, "We will call you and let you know if you passed." But they never called me, because then we got the papers to go to America.

We had filled out the refugee forms in Karago, but we were told we had to pay a lot of money to go to America or Australia or anywhere. We did not have money. We filled out the forms and gave them to the UN. They said if we had no money, we would have to wait. We waited for many years. Then, one day, God smiled on us and the UN called us and told us, "You are on the list to go to America."

We were so excited to hear that we were going to America. First, we had to have interviews. They already had the information, but they asked the questions to see if we would give the right answers. If people do not give the right answers, they don't pass the test. They don't go to America. Each person must know the answers to all the questions. A lot of people fail that test.

They asked us what church we go to. We are Christian, so they matched us with a church that would help our family.

We had to go to the doctor and have physical exams, shots, medicines, everything to make sure we were healthy. If anyone was not healthy, they could not go. We were heathy, so we could go to America. We had a seminar for three days to learn about how to live in America. We learned how to shop, how to meet the neighbors, how to take the bus, and all about American food and money.

Eight people in my family came to America. My oldest brother and sister stayed in Africa, because they did not live with us; they had their own homes.

Each person could bring one bag: clothes, shoes, things like that. We had to leave our animals—our chickens and ducks, goats, and pig. Those we had to sell or give away. Anything that would not fit in a bag had to stay in Africa.

We packed up our things and we were ready. A big bus came to the camp to pick up everyone who was going to the airport. It was a long drive, maybe two hours, to get to the airport. This was our first time in an airport, first time in an airplane. We were excited. The first plane was so small! It took us from Tanzania to Kenya. The next plane was much bigger. We flew from Kenya to Dubai, to France, then New York, then Phoenix, and then to Spokane. Flying was crazy. We were so tired. They gave us food, but we did not eat it because we did not know this food. They gave us ice cream, but we didn't know about ice cream—it was so cold. Now we eat ice cream, but then we did not.

People from the United Methodist Church came to get us at the airport in Spokane. The people from the church took us to the pastor's house, and we stayed there for many months— close to a year. Everyone from the church was so kind to us. They helped us in so many ways. Then the church helped us to find a house. It was hard to find a house for such a big family.

Before we could go to school, we had to go to the clinic for more shots, and we had to get our shots to get our green cards too. We needed our green cards so we could work.

We all started school. My parents went to adult education classes to learn English. My four young siblings went to elementary school. My brother and I went to high school. We rode the bus to school; we did not have to walk. We had lunch at school; we did not have to be hungry. We were so thankful to go to school. We had to learn English and math and computers, everything.

First, we learned the alphabet, and how to introduce ourselves. I made friends. We learned how to get lunch in the cafeteria. After lunch we played soccer together, and my new friends helped me with my homework. In the beginning, I felt like a piece of furniture, like a chair sitting there, not understanding anything. Then I started to learn. Life started to be better.

## Epilogue

In 2015 I got married in the United Methodist Church in Spokane. Now I have my own family. I studied culinary arts at school and found a job in a restaurant. Now I want to be a truck driver, so I am saving money to go to school and get my license. In 2019 I became a citizen. My children and my wife are citizens too. We thank God every day that we are Americans.

# Jeanine

**Congo**
**US Entry: 2010**

Long ago my family was from Rwanda, but I do not remember exactly when they moved to Congo. My mother was born in Congo. I have two older brothers and a younger brother. We were born in Congo too.

In Congo we had a big house and everything we needed. My family—my grandparents, aunties, uncles, and cousins— lived in the same neighborhood. We had relatives in Rwanda too. Sometimes friends and relatives would go back and forth across the border to Rwanda to visit. The land around my home was beautiful, green hills. My parents had good jobs. Life was good and we did not want for anything. We were happy.

Then things started to change. Congo was not safe anymore. Congolese people said people like us who were Tutsi and spoke Kinyarwanda did not belong in Congo. My relatives started leaving, moving to Rwanda and other neighboring countries.

When I was young, my father and two sisters were killed in a conflict because they were Tutsi. Some people got killed over material things. People wanted what we had, and they just took it, no questions asked. My mother realized we had to leave. We took what we could carry and left everything else.

We lived on the Congo side of Lake Kivu, and we needed to cross the lake to go to Rwanda. We had to walk to the lake and try to find a boat to take us across the lake to Rwanda.

People who said they were soldiers stopped people and made them pay to use "their road" or to cross "their bridge." If you had money, you could pay and go on your way, but if you did not have money anything could happen. They would take whatever you had, whatever they wanted. If you didn't have anything, they might kill you.

The journey was frightening. We were so hot, tired, hungry, and thirsty. When you are a refugee you have to keep running, you cannot go back. In some of the places where we were hiding, we would hear guns and noises from miles away, which used to scare us. We thought it could be us next.

We paid to take a boat across the lake. Lake Kivu is a very big lake. The boat was very hot and crowded. There was no food or water on the boat. We were so afraid and too stressed to sleep. Throughout the whole journey we were always praying to God that He would help us reach the other side.

When we arrived in Rwanda, first we stayed in a transit camp. That is a temporary camp. Everyone lived in one huge tent. There was no privacy. We were crowded together. Everyone was afraid, hot, and tired. Everyone had to be interviewed to get into a refugee camp. The interviewers could not tell anyone anything. They just asked questions. At first people thought [living in] the camp was temporary, just until Congo was safe again. We were always praying that one day we would go back to our homes. There were so many groups fighting against each other, though; maybe it will never be safe.

This was before people had cell phones, so we could not just call our relatives to tell them where we were or ask for help. Everyone in the family was scattered. We did not know where anyone was. Some of our family are lost forever.

After a long time, we were sent to Nyabiheke, a brand-new refugee camp. At first, we lived in a tent. The sun would shine on the tent, through the tent walls, and make everything inside hot. Even the water in the water jugs was hot. People started to make mud-and-wattle walls around the tents to keep the tents cooler. The roof was still a tent, but the walls were mud and wattle, like a traditional house.

The government had to figure out what people needed and how to get it to the refugee camps. The government had to figure out how to provide education. The first year there was no school. Then we studied sitting on the ground under the trees. Later we had school outside the camp. UNICEF [the United Nations Children's Fund, a humanitarian agency] gave us backpacks with school supplies, and it was almost like a normal school. We went to school from 8:00 to 3:00 and we went home for lunch. Food was delivered to the camp one time each month: maize, beans, and cooking oil. If people did not manage their food carefully, they might run out before the end of the month. Then their family would go hungry.

In the camp there were people from different places, speaking different languages: Kinyarwanda, Lingala, Kiswahili, French, and other languages from different parts of Congo. People were all different, but everyone had the same situation, so we became close. People came together to help each other. Women helped with the children. There were some jobs in the camp for people to make some money, but no one could work outside the camp. People did not have work papers. Some people traded work for healthy food or things they needed.

My mother was a kindergarten teacher. In the camp she became a counselor, working to help people. Many people had PTSD [post traumatic stress disorder]. Sometimes men would feel useless and frustrated because they could not help their families, and they would get violent. When there was domestic violence, my mother would help women go to a safe place.

We lived like this for a long time. When I was fifteen, we finally got our papers to go to the United States. We packed our things and said goodbye to all of our friends. It was scary and wonderful too. We took many planes to come to America. It seemed to take forever. When we arrived, people from World Relief met us at the airport in Spokane. They helped us find an apartment and gave us wonderful volunteers from church who helped us learn many things about American culture. Despite the language barrier we had, they were kind and welcoming. They made us feel like we belonged somewhere, which was not something we were used to. Then we all started school.

My older brother and I went to high school. Our little brother went to elementary school, and our mother went to night school to learn English. At first, we were worried. How could we go to school when we did not know the language? But at school we had classes to learn English with other students who were learning English. In school we made friends and we learned everything we needed to learn. We also had amazing teachers, especially Mrs. Rouse, who helped us gain the confidence in continuing our education and who encouraged me to go to college. She always told us that here in America you can be anything you want as long as you work hard.

## Epilogue

I graduated from high school and went to college. In June 2019, I graduated with my bachelor's degree in communication. Now I work at World Relief as a case manager. I plan to work for a year then go back to school to get my master's degree in social work. My younger brother is going to college now too. My older brother owns a business in Houston, Texas and is married with children now. We are grateful and happy here in the United States. We still have things in Congo, but we cannot go back for them. Material things are not worth a person's life.

# PART 2

# ASIA

The name Asia may come from the Assyrian word *asu*, meaning "east."

**AREA:** 17.2 million square miles (44.5 million sq. km) (the largest continent)

**POPULATION:** 4.64 billion (the most populous continent; 61 percent of the world population)

**LANGUAGES:** numerous languages, mainly from Sino-Tibetan, Indo-European, and Altaic language families (2,300 languages total)

**RELIGIONS:** Hinduism, Islam, unaffiliated, Buddhism, and more

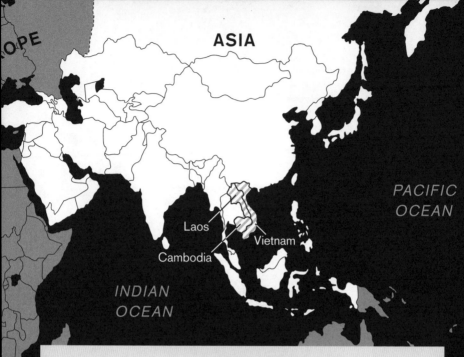

CHAPTER 6

# VIETNAM AND LAOS

....................................................................

## A Few Facts about Vietnam

**AREA:** 127,889 square miles (331,231 sq. km)

**POPULATION:** 97.59 million

**LANGUAGES:** Vietnamese, English, French, Mandarin Chinese, Khmer, and others

**RELIGIONS:** Buddhism, Christianity, Confucianism, Daoism, and Islam

# A Few Facts about Laos

**AREA:** 91,429 square miles (236,800 sq. km)

**POPULATION:** 6.85 million

**LANGUAGES:** Lao, French, and eighty others including Hmong and Khmer

**RELIGIONS:** Buddhism, with local religions, Confucianism, Christianity, Islam, and Baha'i

# A Little History

Trade between Asia and Europe began in ancient times. Europeans wanted Asian spices, gems, and other resources. After the fifteenth century CE, European nations became more powerful and began colonizing parts of Asia. The French occupied southern Vietnam and Laos and formed French Indochina in the nineteenth century. Businesses were owned by the French or other foreigners. The majority of Asian people were poorly paid, had limited rights, and had very little access to higher education.

In the early 1900s, an anticolonial movement started in French Indochina. A Vietnamese man born Nguyen Sinh Cung formed the Indochinese Communist Party. He was known by many names, including Nguyen That Thanh, and became known as Ho Chi Minh, "the Bringer of Light."

During World War II, Japan took control of Vietnam from France. Ho Chi Minh cooperated with the Allies and provided them with information on Japanese movements in Indochina. Ho Chi Minh declared independence in 1945 after the United States beat Japan. France took control of the south. Ho Chi Minh asked the United States and other Western countries to help the Vietnamese people gain independence from France. Without the resources from southern Vietnam, Ho Chi Minh turned to the USSR and Communist China. Vietnam became two separate countries, the Democratic Republic of Vietnam (North Vietnam) and French Indochina (South Vietnam). However, fighting between the two sides continued. Refugees moved to their preferred side.

The United States, worried about communism in Southeast Asia, supported the democratic government of South Vietnam. With US help, South Vietnam expanded its military and industry. US advisers helped train the South Vietnamese military. North and South Vietnam went to war again, and the US military presence in Vietnam increased. In Laos, Hmong people living in the mountains along the border with Vietnam helped guide the US and South Vietnamese soldiers and provided information about North Vietnamese troop movements.

The Hmong people are an ethnic group originally from China and Southeast Asia. The name Hmong (pronounced 'mung') means "free." Since the 1700s, they had farmed in small villages in the hills and mountains of Laos, Vietnam, and Thailand.

The Hmong in Thailand often sided with the Communists and were considered enemies of the Thai government, but in Laos, the Hmong opposed the Communists, assisting South Vietnamese and American soldiers.

In 1975 the North Vietnamese advanced on South Vietnam and the South Vietnamese army retreated. US forces evacuated, with US Navy and South Vietnamese ships taking along as many refugees as they could fit in. The Vietnam War ended in victory for the North Vietnamese Army.

## Why Did People Leave?

When the North gained control of South Vietnam, the North Vietnamese military hunted down people who had worked with the US and South Vietnamese militaries. The North Vietnamese executed an estimated sixty-five thousand people and imprisoned as many as one million.

Leaving was against the law, so people would sneak out of the country, often on small boats that were not safe for ocean travel. An estimated one and a half million people left Vietnam, and between fifty thousand and two hundred thousand died at sea. More than two hundred thousand Hmong fled from Laos to refugee camps in Thailand when the North Vietnamese burned their villages and destroyed their crops. From Thailand, they resettled in Australia, New Zealand, France, Canada, and the United States.

# Trang

**Vietnam**
**US Entry: 1975**

I was born in Saigon [now Ho Chi Minh City], Vietnam. My parents had moved to Saigon from the north long before I was born. I was the sixth of ten children, and I must have been a naïve child, because I really was not aware of how terrible the war was in my country. I did not see dead bodies or hear bombs like people in the rural areas did. We did not have a TV, so I never saw the really drastic events of the war. My life was hopscotch and jump rope. The climate is Vietnam is warm; there are only two seasons—wet and dry—so we could play games outside all the time. My mother insisted that we take naps, and after my nap she would give me a nickel to buy Hi-Ho crackers from the shop next door. They were my favorite snack. My early life in Saigon was good.

Our school was in two shifts, a morning shift and an afternoon shift. I went to the afternoon shift, so in the mornings I would help my mother with her vegetable stand. All of us had assigned chores then. We did not have a choice; we did what the family said. In middle school we were required to take a foreign language, either French or English. I chose English, but I did not like it. English sounds were so hard to make! I did not understand all of the tenses! I hated English grammar.

I was not aware of any plans to leave Vietnam until April 29, 1975. That day I had gone to the temple to see all the people who were coming into Saigon from the countryside. People were pouring into the city, running from the Viet Cong Army.

There were people everywhere. I was so curious, I wandered through the temple just looking at all the people. Fortunately, I had told my parents where I was going before I left the house. In those days we did not have cell phones, so we had to tell people where we were going.

My brother-in-law and my cousin were in the Vietnamese Navy, so they knew what was happening. They came to our house and said, "We have to leave NOW." The family quickly gathered what they could carry, and everyone was asking, "Where is Trang? Where is Trang?" Luckily, they were able to find me right away.

We started toward the harbor where the US Navy ships were waiting. It took us an hour to get to the harbor on foot. People were running everywhere; the streets were packed. People with motorcycles could not get through the crowds of people, so they just dropped their motorcycles and ran with everyone else. Guns were shooting. Missiles were exploding like fireworks. I did not know what was going on. I could not wrap my head around it. Everything was in chaos.

When we reached the harbor, my mother and father said, "You kids go. We will stay here."

My oldest sister said, "Either we all go, or no one goes." The ship was there, so we all went.

The gangways onto the ships were packed. Everyone wanted to leave. Everyone wanted to get on those ships. There were huge ropes dangling from the sides of the ship, and somehow one of my sisters and I ended up hanging onto those ropes, climbing and being pulled up the side of the ship. I lost my flip-flop, and when I tried to grab it, my sister yelled at me, "Forget it!" We had to focus on surviving, we had to stay alive.

On the ship, women and children were being sent to the upper deck, and the men to the lower deck. Somehow, on that huge ship, we all found each other. It was a miracle: The whole family—all ten of us children and both parents—made it onto that ship. So few families made it out together.

People were crowded together like sardines. We couldn't even lie down. We didn't have room to move. The ship took us to the Philippines, but on the way, we ran out of food and water. I was so hungry and thirsty. Someone told us to tap sea water on our lips. We couldn't drink the sea water, but we could make our lips damp.

In the Philippines, we were given military C-rations. I had peanut butter for the first time. Peanut butter and crackers were so good. There was cheese too. It was so good to eat again. There we were transferred to an even bigger ship and taken to Guam. There were not enough toilets on the ship, so they built an outhouse over the rail. It was so scary to look down and see the ocean!

In Guam, people were assigned tents to live in. There we could have chicken, and we could buy Cup of Noodles for a dollar. That chicken was delicious. My older sister was seven or eight months pregnant, so she stayed in a big Quonset hut, but the rest of the family lived in tents. It was very hot and humid, but we could go to the beach and swim. We stayed in Guam for about a month while the officials decided what to do with us. We studied English while we waited. I still hated all the grammar and verb tenses!

From Guam, we flew to Camp Pendleton on a military plane. This was my first airplane ride, sitting on the bench of a military transport plane. We arrived in Camp Pendleton and began our wait for a sponsor. My older sister, her husband, and their baby girl ended up in Houston, Texas. The rest of us waited in Camp Pendleton for eight months. With eleven people in our family it was not easy to find someone willing to

A Quonset hut is a building made of corrugated metal that is shaped like a half cylinder. The rounded roof and corrugated metal make the Quonset hut strong and easy to assemble. They were originally designed for troops during World War II.

sponsor us. Then Saint Joseph's Catholic Church in Colbert, Washington was brave enough to sponsor us.

From Camp Pendleton we flew to Washington on a commercial airliner. When we came out of the plane into the airport in Washington, I saw televisions with the news broadcasts. I listened to them and thought, "I will never be able to speak English like that!" The people on TV spoke so fast!

The church had rented a three-bedroom house for us in Spokane, Washington. We had a room for the seven girls, a room for the two boys, and a room for the parents. We were crowded but also very, very grateful for all the church did for us.

Our names were so hard for Americans to say that I started just saying, "Me number six" and holding up six fingers.

In 1976, there was no English as a Second Language program in the Spokane Public Schools. They had never needed an ESL program before. The schools had to figure out how to teach us and we had to figure out how to learn too. My sisters and I were on our own. Mostly it was sink or swim, but learning was very important to our family. I was fourteen when I started in eighth grade in Spokane. It was a cold and snowy winter, with the snow up to my knees as I walked to school. I did not ask any questions in school. I didn't know how. Once, some students tried to get me to show my middle finger to the teacher. The way they giggled when they said it, I thought that probably that was not good and they were trying to get me in trouble, so I decided not to show my middle finger to the teacher. I spent a lot of time reading and looking up words in the translation dictionary and practicing English on my own. The "th" sound was so hard to make!

In high school, one teacher would take six or seven of us to teach us English. We had workbooks with a Vietnamese translation written in small letters above the English, and that helped. The rest of our classes we took with the English-speaking American students. I took typing and accounting. To graduate from high school, I had to take a foreign language, so I took German too. I managed to graduate, though.

After high school I went to college for a year, and then I got married. I had three children, and my mother took care of the children while I worked two jobs. During the day I worked as a translator-tutor for Spokane Public Schools, helping other English learners. After that, I had a night job. Somehow it all worked out.

In the 1990s, I went back to Vietnam to visit. It was scary, and I was nervous about how people would see me. I wondered what they might do to me because I left and they stayed. Everyone was so poor. Their lives were so much harder than when I lived there. The government had taken everything from them. We returned for another visit in 2000s, and life was much more modern. The economy was improving. There were people who were wealthy, but there were still poor people who were struggling.

What I would like people to know about refugees is how grateful we are to have the chance to have a life. The English language is hard. It is not easy to come to a new country and learn a whole new language and way of life, but we are grateful for what we have been given, for the help we have received.

My husband and I have a comfortable life. We have the basics, everything we really need. We are grateful for our lives here in the United States, for having a roof over our heads, food to eat, and children we are proud of. That is what a successful life is to me. Our children have grown up healthy and happy, with good careers. Now my dream is to retire healthy so I can spend time with our grandchildren.

# Nga

**Vietnam/Cambodia**
**US Entry: 2014**

I was born in Hanoi, Vietnam, but I do not remember Vietnam. I moved to Cambodia with my family when I was one year old. At that time my dad had been arrested by the government of Vietnam because he fought for freedom. The Vietnamese government did not seem to agree with him, so they put him in jail for ten years. When my dad got arrested, my mom decided to take my siblings and me to Cambodia. I do not remember that journey either, because I was so young, but we crossed into Cambodia without papers. We could not get papers because my father was in prison.

Being a single mom who had to take care of small children was not easy. Mom had to face a lot of difficulties in her life to keep us alive. For ten years, she was working so hard to earn the money for our living. We all lived in just one room. She sold street food. When we were little, we could not help her. Later, we could help her sell food. We had no papers so we could not go to school.

One day my dad returned home. When I first saw him, I could not recognize who he was because he had left when I was little. I just stared at him. My mom told me that he was my father. I was so happy; my tears fell down my cheeks. I could not believe that my dad had really returned. He got really emotional and hugged me really tightly.

The police always came to our house looking for my father when we were in Cambodia. After a while, my dad made a decision to move to Thailand, where we thought it would be safer to stay. When we arrived in Thailand, it felt like a new chapter of life just got started. It was like being a baby again. I did not know anything. I did not know the language. I did not know the places. I had to learn a new language, a new culture, and their rules. It was scary too, because we were "illegal." If the police would catch us, they would deport us back to Vietnam and maybe my dad would get arrested again. Maybe we would all go to jail.

We stayed in Bangyai, near Bangkok, Thailand for five years. My father had friends who helped him get a job. My mother worked cleaning the streets. My brother and I still could not go to school. I worked as a dishwasher at a restaurant for 30 bat [about $1] a night. I worked until 5 a.m. I worked with people my age and started to have some friends there. In Cambodia people said bad things about us because we did not have a father. In Thailand we had a family and friends. My brother and I also became hairdressers, which made pretty good money to help our family. We had an apartment and a bicycle.

We registered as refugees with the UNHCR to be relocated to another, safer country. We had to take blood tests to prove that my father was really my father. They thought maybe we were fake children. The DNA test showed that my father was really my father—but my mother was not really my mother. I was so shocked. I never knew. But even though she was not my "real" mother, she was my mother. My brother and I could go with my father, but my mother did not go with us. My mother went back to Cambodia.

Later, we passed our interviews and we had our medical checkups too. We got papers to go to the United States, but because we were in Thailand illegally, we had to go to jail for one week before we could go to the United States. We packed everything we had: a change of clothes, food, a little bit of money. Then the police took us to the airport.

I was excited but a little nervous. My dad was very happy. We flew from Bangkok to Tokyo to Los Angeles to Spokane. I was very, very, airsick the whole way. I was cold and sick; I could not eat anything. We arrived in the night. World Relief met us at the airport and took us to our new apartment. The apartment was much bigger than any place I had ever lived. It had a kitchen with a refrigerator and some food, and a bathroom. We each had a bedroom with beds. In Thailand we had just one room, and everyone just slept wherever they wanted. I did not believe we could drink the water from the faucet without boiling it.

We moved to the United States in 2014. We arrived in Spokane in the summer, but I still felt cold. Everything was so different. Spokane is so quiet. There are no food stands on the streets; there are hardly any people on the streets. The food is so different.

The first day we just stayed in the house and slept. World Relief volunteers came to help us do paperwork and get jobs, and they took us to get shots. Everything was confusing. We had to learn about the buses and shopping for food. We did not recognize anything in the grocery store. We did not know how to read English, so how could we know what was in the packages? Then they took us to the Best Asian Grocery, and we found food we knew.

At age eighteen, I was like a baby again, and I had to start my life new again. World Relief took us to the adult education school for language classes. My father said, "I want my daughter to have an education." So when school started, they took me to high school. I began my freshman year in high school. They put me in a beginner level English class at the Newcomer

Center. Learning a new language was difficult for me—especially when I did not know what the words meant in any language. I made friends at school, really good friends. I had never been to school, so I had so much to learn.

## Epilogue

After three years, I had to leave high school because I was 21, too old for high school. I had to find a new school to continue my education. At that time, I felt so sad and wanted to give up. I thought there was no way for me to continue my education and complete my goal. Education is really important to me and my family. Without degrees a person is not be able to have a good job and decent pay in the future. Without an education a person cannot have a career. That is the reason I started to put myself back together.

The summer of 2017 I took more ESL classes. Then I started my high school completion classes at Spokane Community College. I finished my high school diploma, then started working on my AA [Associate in Arts] degree. I graduated with my AA in 2020. Although my classes were hard, I never gave up. I passed all my classes and reached my goal. In the United States there is so much opportunity. No matter how old people are, they can still go back to school.

I live in Seattle now and have a son. I will keep following my dream to the end. I want to be a useful person so I can help my family and make my family proud of me. I would like to own my own business someday. I would like to travel all over the United States too. When my children grow up, I would love for them to follow my footsteps.

# Nou Vang

**Hmong/Laos**
**US Entry: 1989**

I am Hmong, from Laos, and this is my story.

The Hmong have a long tradition of needlework: embroidery, quilting, and a reverse applique called Pa' nDau [flower cloth]. In refugee camps, the Hmong created story cloths, large wall hangings and quilts depicting scenes of their flight from Laos and their lives in the refugee camps. Men drew the stories on cloth, and then women stitched and embroidered them.

When my parents were married, my grandmother pretended to chase my father away. She said, "No, you cannot have my daughter! She is precious to me! You cannot take her." This is the tradition of the Hmong people. The family must show the husband that his wife is special, that they love her, so he will love her too.

Then the family had a feast and celebrated their marriage.

My family were farmers. Sometimes my father would go to hunt in the jungle.

In 1975, the war against the Hmong people started. Vietnamese soldiers came to kill the Hmong people. They dropped bombs, burned the villages, burned the fields, and killed people because the Hmong helped the American soldiers in the war in Vietnam.

One day my uncle said, "It is not safe here. We must go." My father and mother packed everything they could carry. My father carried my little sister; my mother carried food and our cooking pots. I was too little to carry anything. I was so small.

My family and my uncle's family went through the jungle to another village and stayed there for a little while. Still we were not safe. We traveled again. We moved from place to place. We tried to stay away from the Vietnamese soldiers. In the jungle we would eat the food we found, like wild potatoes.

One day, my father was looking for food, and the Vietnamese soldiers shot him. They killed him.

My uncle said, "We cannot live here. We must go to Thailand." We traveled through the jungle. I was lucky; I was eight years old, and my sister was four years old. If we were younger, the adults would have given us opium to make us quiet. If the babies cry, the soldiers can find us, and kill us, so people would mix opium in water and give it to the babies to make them sleep. But this was very dangerous. They did not know how much to give, so sometimes the babies died. My sister and I were old enough to be quiet, the adults did not give us opium. We were scared all the time.

My mother married another man, my stepfather. We traveled to try to get to Thailand. We had to cross the Mekong River. The soldier tried to stop Hmong people from crossing the river. They would kill Hmong people who tried to cross the river and leave their bodies in the jungle for the porcupines to eat their bones.

Many people did not know how to swim. They cut bamboo and tied it together to help them float across the river. Some people would float with inner tubes. Sometimes, if one person could swim, they would pull the others across the river. We were lucky. A canoe came to take us across the river.

In 1981, we made it to Thailand. Thai people stopped us. They patted us all over to make sure we did not have any weapons. They searched our belongings. They took our knives and anything metal. Any money people had, the soldiers took. My mother had sandals; she had cut the bottom of the sandals and hid a little money in her sandals.

At that time, my mother was pregnant. When the time came to have the baby, my mother died, and the baby died. Now I was with my uncle's family, my little sister, and my stepfather. Soon my step-father married again. Then I was with my stepfather, my stepmother, my sister, and my stepbrother.

We lived in the Ban Vinai Thai Refugee Camp. We tried to farm here too. There was a school, but we had to pay school fees. We had to buy school supplies. My stepparents would not pay for me. I went to school one year, then I had to go to work. I worked on the farm. Then I learned to sew and embroider, and I worked making purses and cloth to sell. I could not go to school.

In 1987, we did the paperwork to go to America. We had to have interviews and raise our hands to say, "Yes, we want to go to America." If we do not say we want to go to America, they would take us back to Laos.

Then a big bus took us to Bangkok. In Bangkok we studied how to live in America. We had to learn how to use doors and American toilets. We learned how to make sandwiches, how to eat American food. We studied for maybe seven months.

At that time, we had to have medical tests to prove we were not sick. If we did not have any disease, we can could to America. If we were sick, we would have to stay in Thailand.

I was a teenager when we flew to Fresno, California. Everything was different in America. My stepparents told me I had to get a job or get married. English was still hard; I couldn't find

a job. I didn't know how to fill out the applications. I did not know what to do.

I prayed. I said, "God, you know me. I am here living with my stepparents. I don't know what to do. Please help me." I was afraid. It was a very dark time for me. I worried,

*What if I marry a man who does not love me, and my life gets even worse? What if I get married and have children, and get divorced, then I have an even harder time than when I was single?* I prayed every night.

At that time, my [future] husband's wife had gone away. He was living in Spokane with three children and his mother. He came to Fresno, and he met my auntie. She asked him, "Why did you come to Fresno?"

He said, "I have come to look for a wife."

My auntie said, "I know a girl. She is living with her step-parents. They do not really love her, but she is a good girl. If you marry her, she will be a good wife for you."

At that time, we had not met. We had never seen each other. He came to Fresno and talked to families with daughters. He talked to a family with a daughter, but she was not ready to get married. He talked to another family. They had a daughter, but she was not ready to get married either. Then he remembered what my auntie had said. He got my phone number.

He called me on the phone, and we talked. He said, "I know you are looking for love for a long time. If you will marry me, I will love you forever."

We got married. Then he told me he had three children. He brought me back to Spokane. I started to go to high school, learning English and everything for a high school diploma. It was not easy. When I got home, I had homework to do but no one to help me. Also, I was learning how to be a good mother to our children. I wanted to be a good mother. I was afraid I would not know how to be a good mother, but I wanted to be a kind and good mother. I wanted to love my husband's children like my own child, the way my mother and father loved me before they died. I wanted a happy family.

# Epilogue

I have been married to my husband for 27 years now. We help each other. We are not the boss of each other; we help each other. We are happy together. We have ten children—six boys and four girls—and seven grandchildren. I finished my high school diploma. I am a citizen now. My children know we came here to give them a better life. They know they must work and be honest to have a good life in America. We did not come here to take from America. We came, and people helped us. Now we must give back to America and help others.

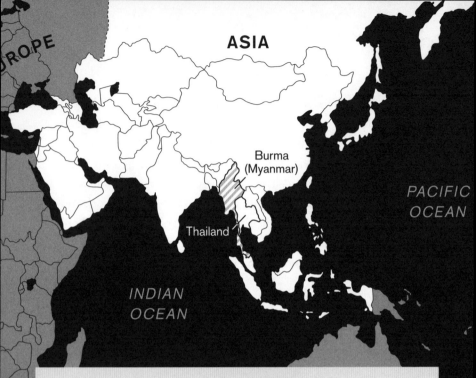

CHAPTER 7

# BURMA (MYANMAR)

## A Few Facts about Burma (Myanmar)

**AREA:** 261,219 square miles (676,554 sq. km)

**POPULATION:** 54.8 million

**LANGUAGES:** Burmese and other Indigenous languages

**RELIGIONS:** Buddhism, Christianity, Islam, and Animism

# A Little History

The population of Burma (Myanmar) consists of 135 diverse ethnic groups with their own languages and cultures. Ethnic Burmese make up 68 percent of the population. The next largest group are the ethnic Shan, who make up about 10 percent of the population. Indian and Chinese cultures have influenced the country's culture ever since ancient trade routes between China and India first ran through northern Burma.

In 1511 the Portuguese arrived on the Malay Peninsula and opened up trading with Europe and the rest of Asia. By 1612 the British East India Company claimed Burma. The Burmese resisted colonization, but the Anglo-Burmese War (1824–1826) resulted in the British taking control.

The British lived comfortable lives in Burma and became wealthy from Burma's resources, but the people of Burma did not share in this wealth. In the 1920s and 1930s the people of Burma protested British rule.

Burma was an important battleground in World War II. The Allies needed Burma to supply their troops in the Pacific, but they had to fight Japan for control of the country.

In 1948 Burma declared independence from Britain. Tensions surfaced between the ethnic Burmese and other ethnic groups. The Burmese government limited civil rights such as free speech. The Burmese military attacked the villages of ethnic minorities and destroyed their food supplies. People who protested government policies were arrested, and many unarmed protesters were killed.

The internal conflicts that began at independence have continued. In 1989 the country's military leaders changed its name from Burma to the Republic of the Union of Myanmar. But many countries still use the name Burma because they believe the Myanmar government violates the human rights of its people.

## Why Do People Leave?

The government of Myanmar, which is controlled by ethnic Burmese, has used violence to push ethnic minorities out of their homes. These ethnic minorities do not trust the government of Myanmar to allow them to live in safety and peace.

# Eh Kler

**Myanmar**
**US Entry: 2008**

I don't know exactly where I was born, but it was in Thailand, across the border from Burma. My family is from the Karen State of Burma. Some people call it Myanmar. My dad came from the city, but my mom grew up out in the rural areas, in the jungle with bamboo trees all around.

I was the second child in my family. I have an older sister who is smart and always does what she is supposed to do. I am not like her; I don't like anyone telling me what to do. I am the only boy in our family. I always wanted a brother. I have one sister who was born in the US, so she could be president someday.

When I was little, we had to move a lot. The Burmese soldiers would come over the border into Thailand and burn down the Karen refugee camps, burn all the houses, all the food, and kill people.

In the refugee camps, we had to work for everything. We had to pump water with a hand pump and carry it to our house. I carried the water buckets with a bamboo pole over my shoulders. To cook, we had to collect firewood. Twice a month we would get rations of rice and beans. Each family would get just so much, depending on how many people were in the family.

Our houses were made of bamboo and leaves, we didn't have electricity when I lived in the camp. Now people have sheet metal roofs and they are getting electricity, and some people even have TVs.

In the refugee camp, I would wake up in the morning, get dressed, and go to school. The school building was made of concrete blocks and had a metal roof. During the week it was a school, but on Sunday it was the church.

School was not like American schools. Teachers spanked kids there. We used small black chalkboards to write, instead of paper. We had long benches and tables, not desks. We would say a pledge to the Karen People at the beginning and end of the school day.

After school we would play. When it rained, the rain was warm, and we would strip down to our underwear and run in the rain, play and slide in the mud. We had lots of fun.

Once some Canadians came and built a playground for us. They gave us gift boxes with clothes, shoes, toothbrushes, and soap—all the things people need every day. Then they gave people haircuts and medical checkups. Then we put on a talent show before they went home, to thank them. My dad still has that shirt. It is a pretty nice shirt.

We didn't really like the Thai people. They had money and everything, but they didn't help us or share with us. My family decided we needed to leave Thailand because we couldn't really have a life there. My grandmother applied with the refugee organization UNHCR, and our turn came when I was eight, almost nine years old. I never knew we would come to America; I never really knew anything about America before we came here.

When we found out we were going to America, we started packing. We packed everything we had, but then we were told we couldn't take that much with us, so we had to give away a lot of our stuff.

Grandmother, my parents, my three sisters, and I left the camp together. A bus came to pick us up from the camp and took us into the city. We slept in a hotel for the first time. Everything was so different. We didn't know even how to use a TV. The next morning the bus came and took us to the airport. I didn't even know enough to be scared about plane crashes.

Along the way we met other people who were coming to America, but we didn't know where we were going. We knew we were going to America but not where in America. Dad bought gum on the plane to keep our breath fresh, because we didn't know how long we would travel or how we would stay clean.

The first plane was fancy; the seats had TV screens. The food on the airplane was nasty, though. No one could eat it. It was not like anything we had ever eaten. I was thinking, "What is this? What are you feeding us?" We just drank water while we were traveling.

We got off and on a lot of planes. We flew from Thailand to Tokyo to Los Angeles to Seattle and then to Spokane. The last plane was so small.

When we arrived in Spokane it was late at night. An America family met us at the airport. They took us to their home, fed us, and helped us that first night. They put a movie on the TV for us to watch: *Finding Nemo*. It was the first movie I ever saw.

The next day, some Karen people who already lived in Spokane and the pastor from the Karen church came and got us and took us to our new home, one part of a triplex house. They helped us get food and everything we needed. They took us to the Best Asian Market, and we got food that we knew how to eat.

People were so good to us. People we didn't even know helped us and gave us things we needed.

We had a TV but no DVD player, and a nice guy was so generous—he gave us a DVD player to keep and gave us a DVD of *The Cat in the Hat* too.

Our first days were so happy. We had so much. We could eat a lot and watch TV and be in a warm place. The house was so nice—we loved it! Before we came to America, we never had a house with glass windows and doors, a house that was not easy to burn down. We never had a house with faucets and hot water.

Soon the snow started to fall, and I was thinking about making snow cones with the snow, like we sometimes got in Thailand—the shaved ice that you put flavored syrup on? The snow was so beautiful and clean and white. Then more snow and more snow kept falling. It was so cold, and the snow was taller than me! Snow was not as nice as it looked.

Life in Spokane was pretty confusing sometimes. Getting places was confusing. We had to take this bus at this time to that bus and change buses; it was easy to get lost. Transportation was hard. The language, the way people talked, was even harder. Everything was so different and so confusing.

We didn't really know much about America when we arrived here, but we thought everyone in America would have everything they need, everyone would be healthy and happy. We didn't expect to see homeless people or dirty places. We thought everything would be nice and beautiful.

Pretty soon I was registered for school, and I went straight into fourth grade at Grant Elementary. I didn't know any English, so sometimes when the other kids were doing lessons, I worked with a special teacher in the classroom. I did different work than the other kids. I read a lot of Curious George books; I guess the teacher really liked Curious George. She had a George puppet she would make talk when she was reading.

School was hard because I did not know English. I didn't know the same things the American kids knew. I didn't know what to say, how to say it. Classroom teachers never listened, they never had patience with the students who were still learning English. Once I wanted to ask an American student to come to me, and I used the wrong finger. The kid told the teacher, and I got a pink slip. The teacher did not understand that I didn't know about The Finger. In our country all fingers are the same.

Some kids who didn't speak English didn't want to go to school. The other refugee kids and I didn't know what to wear, how to act. Sometimes the American kids would laugh because we got it wrong. We felt stupid because we didn't know how to speak English, but my ELD teacher made me want to be there. The ELD teacher helped me a lot. She listened to me and she made it fun. We got a sticker for coming to class on time and if we came to school on time every day for two weeks, we got to pick a prize from the prize basket.

Making friends with American kids and learning the language helped make life easier. I learned to speak a lot faster than I learned reading and writing. Having friends helped a lot.

Sometimes I had bad examples that had a bad influence on me. Some people used bad language and taught us bad language that got us in trouble.

In middle school, I got angry easily. I talked back. But then in high school, I met teachers who really listened—and then I started to listen too. I didn't want to go to jail, I didn't want to be homeless. I realized I had to change my ways. I started really thinking about what I wanted to do in life. I made good American friends. I started working and earning money to help my family.

## Epilogue

Now that I have graduated from high school, I am working and planning to go to college. Maybe I will be a barber, or maybe a therapist who can help other young people get their lives together. It is hard to decide. I learn best when I do things with my hands, but I want to help other people.

I want to get married and have a family. I want to earn enough money to support my family. I want a job that will let me spend time with my own kids.

A lot of American kids take a lot for granted. America has a lot to give us, it just takes a while for it to sink in. America helps us with a lot of stuff, but a person has to put in effort too. If you aren't willing to get up and get to work, why would anyone want to pay you? The American dream is out there, but you have to work to get it.

# Mar Nay

**Myanmar**
**US Entry: 2008**

Explore Burma!
You can walk in the jungle.
You can see beautiful waterfalls, butterflies, and flowers.
You can see elephants and beautiful birds.
You can see dead bodies in the trees.
Watch out for tigers, snakes, and soldiers.
Dress for hot weather.
Don't forget to bring your binoculars and camera!

My family is from Burma, but I was born in Maw Ker Refugee Camp in Thailand. That refugee camp is not there anymore. When I was young, maybe seven or eight, we had to move to the Umpiem Refugee Camp because one day the Burmese soldiers came and attacked our camp with rockets and guns. It was a normal day—then suddenly, there were bombs exploding everywhere. Rockets were coming out of the sky. People were running, screaming, and crying. People were looking for their children, because the children had been playing. They did not know the Burmese soldiers would attack. Many people were injured. People died.

United Nations trucks came to help us move. We had to take the houses apart, bring what we could fit on the truck. Each family could only have one truck, one trip. If something didn't fit on the truck it had to stay behind.

When we moved to Umpiem, it was just jungle. We saw wild animals, monkeys, and birds. We had to build the camp—build the houses and dig a well for water to drink. In Maw Ker we had our own house, and my grandparents had their own house, and my uncle had his own house. When we moved to Umpiem, we had to combine the building materials of our houses to make one house. Later the UN brought us more bamboo to build with, but it was not enough to build big houses. The Thai government took half of everything.

The UN would send us rice to eat, but the Thai government would take half the rice. We never had enough to eat. We would hunt for whatever we could find to eat. We hunted birds with a slingshot. We picked vegetables in the jungle, and bananas, but there was never enough to eat. There were no fat people in the camp.

In the camp we had no medicine. If a person was sick or injured, they might die—50/50 chance.

There were a lot of snakes that if they bite you, you will die. One time when I was picking vegetables, I didn't see that there was a snake. I was just looking for vegetables. I saw a frog. I thought about catching that frog, but I decided to keep picking vegetables. Then the frog moved, and then the snake moved. That is when I saw the snake. If the frog had not moved, maybe the snake would have bitten me. Then I would be dead.

We could not leave the camp. If you leave the camp, the Thai soldiers would arrest you and put in jail for many days, and they would not give you food. But sometimes people would sneak out of the camp to go hunting, to find food.

Life in the camp was hard, but we had fun too. For fun, we played a game with marbles. We dug little holes, then we would use our fingers to shoot one marble to hit another marble into a hole. Marbles were expensive for us, but this was a fun game. We played a game like dodgeball, but with throwing our shoes instead of balls. We didn't have real shoes, we only had flip-flops. Our flip-flops were old, thin, and worn out. We sewed them together when they broke.

When we wanted to come to America, we had to fill out a lot of paperwork. So many people wanted to leave the camps, to go to Australia or Canada or America. We had to wait a long time to get our interviews. Everyone in the family had to be interviewed. They would ask many questions. In the interviews they would ask if anyone in the family had been in the army. If someone was in the army, their family could not come to America. They tried to trick people into saying that someone in the family was in the army. No one who had been a soldier could go to America.

The leader in our area announced the names of the people who were approved to go to America. When our names were called, I was so happy!

We had to go to the city for medical tests. If people were sick, if they had any disease, they could not come to America. They could get medicine and then go through the whole process again: interviews and everything.

In the city they gave us good food. I ate so much.

After we passed our physicals, we went back to the camps and packed everything we could take. Since we did not have shoes, the UN gave us all shoes; everyone wore the same kind of shoes. My new shoes didn't really fit well. They were a little tight, and I got blisters on my feet.

The Thai people tried to scare us. They told us that in America people would kill us and feed us to the crocodiles. One of my uncles was already in America. He called us on the camp phone station and told us, "Don't worry. People in America are good."

Before we left, we did not have a party, but we had a church service to pray that we would all be okay. My grandparents had to stay behind; they came later with my other uncle.

My grandfather spoke English. He had worked with American soldiers when he was young. No one else in the family could speak English.

When we got to the airplane, I was so happy, so excited! I was too excited to buckle my seatbelt, too excited to sleep! I looked out of the window. People talked to us, but I didn't understand anything. Maybe they were telling me not to open the window because people were sleeping, I do not know. We did not know how to tell the people on the plane what we wanted to eat or drink. We just drank water.

When we landed in Spokane, landing was scary and bouncy. Everything was so strange. I felt dizzy and wobbly. My uncle Moonlight and the people from World Relief were there to meet us. My uncle and his family were the first Karen people to come to Spokane.

I was so happy and so tired. World Relief had rented a house for us. When I came to America everything was different. My uncle had to come and teach us how to do everything: how to turn on the faucets for cold and hot water, how to push the buttons to make the stove work, how to make the house warm. We never had anything like that before.

A few weeks later my father went to work. He got a job making pizza. He had to work to pay for the house and everything. We had to learn how to shop for food. There was so much to learn.

Then I went to school. In the cafeteria, I ate everything. I loved all the food. I loved hamburgers. I loved pizza. I think I gained a lot of weight when I came to school. I was scared of the classroom—I didn't know anything. In the school in the camp, if students could not answer a question, the teacher would hit the students or throw things at them. I could not speak English so I was afraid the teachers would be mad at me. It was scary.

Sometimes, I went into the bathroom and cried. School was hard. There was so much to learn. I missed my friends in the refugee camp.

After a while, things got better. My teachers were kind to me. I learned English. I took art and photography classes. That was so cool. I learned how to use a computer. I learned American history, math, and science. I made new friends. Spokane is my home now. I think I will live here forever now.

## Epilogue

I am an American citizen now. I am married. I have two daughters. I work and support my family. I help my community and my church. I teach Karen children to play guitar and sing Karen songs. In the future I hope to keep my culture, and help my daughters know what it is like to be in a refugee camp, so they can understand and have empathy. I try to be a good leader in my community and church, to help people the best way I can.

We came here for a reason. If we stayed in our country, we would be dead. We might have starved to death or the soldiers might have killed us. We had no food; we had no future. We came here to have a future. We work hard. We share our hospitality. We are good people. Even when we have nothing, we will help anyone.

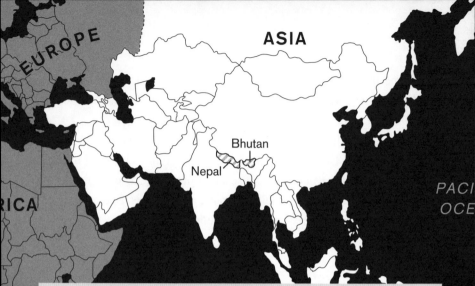

EUROPE

ASIA

Bhutan

Nepal

PACI
OCE

RICA

## CHAPTER 8

# BHUTAN AND NEPAL

### A Few Facts about Bhutan

**AREA:** 14,824 square miles (38,394 sq. km)

**POPULATION:** 752,900

**LANGUAGES:** Dzongkha, Tibetan dialects, and Nepalese dialects

**RELIGIONS:** Buddhism and Hinduism

### A Few Facts about Nepal

**AREA:** 56,827 square miles (147,181 sq. km)

**POPULATION:** 30 million

**LANGUAGES:** Nepali, Maithili, Bjojpuri, and many others

**RELIGIONS:** Hinduism, Buddhism, Islam, and Kirat

# A Little History

The Himalayan Mountains kept Bhutan and Nepal isolated for most of their history. There is a cultural connection between India and Nepal, and the majority of Nepali today are Hindu. Bhutan is more connected to Tibet and China, and the majority of Bhutanese are Buddhist.

In the 1600s, the rulers of Bhutan invited craftspeople from Nepal to come to Bhutan. During the nineteenth century, they welcomed more Nepali people to the southern part of the country while Britain was colonizing India. Bhutan, with its tiny population, needed more workers. People from Nepal settled on the southern plain of Bhutan.

The southern plains are the main agricultural area of Bhutan, so these people became prosperous farmers. They became known as the Lhotshampa, "people of the south." The Lhotshampa continued to speak Nepali but considered themselves Bhutanese.

After conflicts with China and Britain, Bhutan signed a treaty with Britain in 1865, which ceded territory from Bhutan on their southern border and established free trade between British-colonized India and Bhutan.

After World War II, India became independent from Britain and in 1949 signed a treaty with Bhutan. India allowed Bhutan to run its own government.

Bhutan was a multicultural country until 1985, when the Bhutanese king decreed that Bhutan would be "One Nation, One People." New laws prohibited the Lhotshampa from speaking Nepali or wearing their traditional clothes. Protests against the new laws were considered treason, and thousands of Nepali-speaking Lhotshampa were arrested, imprisoned, tortured, and even killed.

Many Nepali-speaking people were deported from Bhutan. Thousands traveled to Nepal, seeking refuge. Nepal no longer recognized them as Nepali citizens, but the United Nations High Commissioner for Refugees set up refugee camps in Nepal. Between 1990 and 2016, Nepal hosted 120,000 Bhutanese refugees.

## Why Did People Leave?

After the "One Nation, One People" decree, life for the Nepali-speaking Lhotshampa became difficult and dangerous. Many were forced out of the country. Government officials and soldiers came into Lhotshampa communities and told them they had a few days to pack up and leave. Their land, businesses, and homes were taken over by their non-Nepali-speaking neighbors.

# Saila Tochhang

**Bhutan**
**US Entry: 2010**

My parents were born in Bhutan. My grandparents were born in Bhutan. My family is from Bhutan.

I was born in the village of Shivalaya, Sibsoo in southern Bhutan. The name has been changed since then to a name that sounds less Nepali and more Dzongka. (Dzongka is the official language of Bhutan.)

When I was young, on a normal day, I would wake up early and do my morning chores: fetch water, care for the animals, and then have my breakfast. Breakfast was porridge sometimes, or whatever my mother cooked. Then we would walk, about 1 to 1 ½ hours, to school. School began with a morning assembly, and then we went to class. In school the teacher was the boss, with no questions. The teachers could discipline us however they wished. Whatever the teacher said or did was okay, as long as there weren't any broken bones. Some schools had lunch served, but others did not. We were often hungry at school. At 3:00 or 3:30, we walked home again. We had a snack and did our chores, then had an early dinner. We did our homework and then went to sleep. We had no electricity, just an oil lamp. Sometimes we would stay up and talk. My father told good stories, traditional tales or funny memories.

My childhood was happy. We had no worries. We were happy with small things, traditional games, playing with toys we made. The community came together for festivals and celebrations. Everyone in our village was connected in some way.

Everyone knew each other. Any adult could correct a child; all adults were like parents. I was a happy student, dreaming of a career and a better life.

In the south, we were called "Lhotshampa" to distinguish us from people from Nepal. Our community spoke Nepali and wore Nepali clothes. Nepali was taught in the schools and used in everyday life. In the north, people had originally come from Tibet. They had a different culture, religion, customs, and language. In the north the climate was much colder than in the south, so their clothing was different, made of wool to keep people warm.

After 1988, the government outlawed Nepali dress and language. We had to wear the northern clothing, but it was very uncomfortable because our climate was too warm for those clothes. If people did not follow the dress code, they were fined. If they spoke Nepali in public, they were fined.

People protested. We just wanted to live our lives as humans with rights, but the government arrested people. Anyone who spoke against the new laws was arrested. Thousands of people were arrested. People were sent to prison, tortured, sometimes killed. People disappeared. This forced people to seek shelter in India, but India had a very close relationship with the Bhutan government. They did not want to disrupt that relationship, so they did not want these protestors in India. They took them and dumped them on the border with Nepal.

When I was in high school, I went to boarding school. We had secondary school for grades 9 and 10, then we took a test. If we passed, we went to senior secondary school. When I was in tenth grade, I came home from school for a vacation, for a holiday. I did not know anything about protests against the government, but as it happened, I came home at the same time as a group was protesting. I was arrested and sent to prison, to a labor camp in the north. I had no idea why.

In prison I was tortured. We were chained together in shackles. We were given big hammers to break big rocks into smaller rocks and pile those rocks. We were preparing the rocks to build a new prison. There were thousands of us. We did not have enough food. We slept on the floor with little protection from the cold and the snow. I became very sick, but they did not give me medicine. One of my friends was shot dead, trying to escape, and another went insane.

After eighteen months, they released me. They would release 325 people at a time. They just dropped us off on the street, with no money and no food, our clothes just rags. Somehow I managed to make my way home. When I arrived home, my skin was discolored from my illness, and I was so thin, my mother did not recognize me.

After I came home, I had to report to the police station each week and provide free labor for the whole day. I could only walk from place to place, I was prohibited from using public transportation, and I could no longer go to school. I lived in the village, helping my parents, doing what work I could do.

Finally, I had to flee. I walked to India, and from there I took a bus with a "grandfather," an older man I met who pretended to be my grandfather and took me to Nepal, and then went back to India while I made my way to a refugee camp for Bhutanese people. I was nineteen years old, and alone. I did not register with UNHCR as a refugee, but I lived in the refugee camp, going from hut to hut helping people with whatever I could do, and eating with people who would feed me.

After two months, my parents were given the choice of bringing me home to be arrested again or leaving the country. My family had a home, a house and land, livestock and fields. They left everything. They let the animals loose and left the door open behind them. My mother took some of her jewelry. Everything else, they left behind.

In the camp we registered with UNHCR. I was the only one who could work. My parents needed medical help. My father developed a breathing problem. I took care of them. I built huts in the camp from bamboo. UNHCR helped with rice and lentils, and tarps for the roofs. In the wind, men would have to hold on to the tarps to keep them from blowing away. When the rain blew sideways, the huts would be cold and wet, but we were alive.

My two elder brothers tried to stay in Bhutan, to continue to work. Both of them were teachers in government schools. One was an elementary teacher and the other was a high school science teacher. However, since I was arrested, they were told they could no longer teach. They had to leave Bhutan. My other brother's wife worked for the government, but she was also told she had to leave Bhutan. Because I had been arrested, they could not get their certificate of "No Objection" that would allow them to continue in their jobs. They lost everything. They had to leave everything behind them and joined my parents in Nepal.

I was given a job teaching lower kindergarten in the camp because I knew English, but I didn't know anything about teaching! Then Irish Aid started a program to help train teachers in the refugee camps in Nepal. They taught us to be teachers, like a Montessori program. There was corporal punishment in the camp schools, but there started to be a little less of that as more and more teachers received trainings.

At first, we had school in the open, on the ground, when the weather was good. The next year we built a bamboo building with a thatched roof. We had no furniture, though; students still sat on the ground. There were sixty students to one teacher. In a camp with 20,000 people we had one school.

Later, we had ten schools. The camp was divided into sectors A through I, and each sector had schools. By now I was 20, maybe 21, and I was learning to be a school administrator, supervising eleven other teachers. The Bhutanese Refugee Education Program [BREP] organized the schools and exams, with the support of the Nepal government. Australian volunteers with the Caritas organization helped us.

Through correspondence school, I was able to finish my secondary education, and then I continued to work on my education. I went to Katmandu [the capital of Nepal] for a workshop, and ended up taking a master's exam. I began a program to earn my master's degree.

The Bhutanese refugee camps in Nepal were not like the camps in some countries. We did not have barbed wire fences preventing us from leaving. The government did not give us work permits to work in Nepal, but refugees could easily sneak out of camp to work outside since the camps were not heavily guarded. The camps began to suffer from "brain drain"—that is, people who were educated began to leave the camps. We wanted to go back to our home, Bhutan, but we realized that this would not be possible. People began to get jobs other places, in Nepal and in India. I met and married another teacher. We moved to Katmandu to teach.

In 2007, the UNHCR began to resettle Bhutanese refugees to other countries. My brothers were selected to move to the United States. My father had passed away from asthma. My mother passed away as well.

My wife and I left Katmandu and returned to the refugee camp to do the paperwork to go to the United States. We went through the screening process, had our health checks and background checks, and took the oath. We were able to prove that we could work in the United States. Finally, we received our travel documents and were ready to go. By this time, we also had a four-year-old son. IOM helped us every step of the way.

We landed in Newark, New Jersey on February 12, 2010. The weather was very snowy, so we were not able to leave Newark until February 16. We arrived in Spokane February 16, 2010.

Although I spoke English, everything was strange and different. We had lost all of our social contexts. I could see things and hear things happening but still not really know what was going on. I felt lonely in the crowd. There was so much to do, but I didn't know where to begin.

I found work as a substitute teacher in April, and then I was hired to be a bilingual specialist interpreting for and tutoring students who were learning English. Slowly, we began to build a life for ourselves, to make friends and learn our way. That fall, our son started kindergarten.

Now my son is in high school. We have a little daughter, born in the United States. We have a home. My dream for the future is that my children will never experience what I have experienced, that they will never suffer injustice. I want them to have better lives than I have lived, to do better than I have.

## Epilogue

I still feel the injustice of what was taken from me and my family. A big chunk of my life was taken from me. My home, my citizenship, my heritage were stolen from me, and nothing can substitute for that loss. I wish that someday someone will be able to get justice for the Bhutanese people, and to question the world, "Why did you let this happen?"

Bhutan is known as a democratic nation with a Gross National Happiness Index, but there is no freedom there.

# Bikash

**Nepal**
**US Entry: 2013**

I was born in Jhapa Refugee Camp in Nepal, but my family is from Bhutan. Long ago Bhutan invited Nepali people to come to Bhutan to help them protect their country from the British. In the 1990s Bhutan decided to kick the Nepali people out of Bhutan. The government did not allow Nepali clothes or Nepali language anymore. My grandparents had a big farm, a house three stories tall, and a store. Then Bhutanese people came and burned down their store. They left with other Bhutanese-Nepali people and became refugees in Nepal. They had to just leave everything they owned and walk away.

When I was six years old, my mother went to another refugee camp and father moved to India. They left me with my grandparents. I lived with my grandparents from that time. Sometimes other children would bully me and say I must be a very bad person for my parents to leave me, but I was just a little kid. I didn't do anything to make my parents leave, they just left.

In Jhapa, refugees could leave the refugee camp to go to work. My grandparents went to a farm to work. They also did spinning, making thread and yarn, for money. Sometimes I would help them. We had a goat and rabbits. I would go to the jungle to harvest grass to feed them. We had a food allowance of lentils and rice, but it was not really a lot of food. We could get potatoes and greens from the farm, and we ate rabbit, and we milked the goats. In my religion we do not eat meat, but when you have nothing to eat, you eat whatever you can. Now

I would not eat rabbit meat, or any meat, but there I ate meat when we had meat.

When I was eleven years old, I decided to go to live with my father in India. Life with my father was not easy. He did not give me anything. I walked two hours to school. My father did not give me money for lunch, so I had only breakfast and an evening meal. I was not happy living with my father, so I went back to my grandparents. I left without even saying goodbye.

The refugee camp was a crowded and busy place. There were rules: no drinking and no fighting. When I came back from India, I was shocked by the police presence in the camp. The camp was changing.

When I was sixteen, my grandparents and I were approved for relocation. We were going to the United States. We packed everything we had. I did not have very much, because I never had money to get stuff. I had one backpack of clothes and one gold earring that I someday I will give to my child. The International Organization for Migration (IOM) bus came to the camp market, in front of the police department. Everyone was crying when we got on the bus. I did not have very much, but I gave my money, 20 rupees, to our neighbor family because they had little kids. I felt like I needed to give something to help others because I had this opportunity to leave and have a good life.

My grandparents, an uncle, and I rode the bus to Damak, Nepal. We spent six months there doing interviews and orientation. They gave us a place to stay and chai and biscuits in the morning, daal bhat (lentil curry) and rice in the evening.

Then we got our tickets to the United States. We took a bus to the airport, and finally we flew away from Nepal. We flew from Nepal to Dubai, where we spent ten hours. We did not have a room or anything there; we just slept on the floor. Then we flew to Chicago, Salt Lake City, and finally Spokane.

Traveling made us really tired. The food was different, not like anything we had ever tried. We could not eat it. In Chicago a huge, tall white man said, "Congratulations! Welcome to America!" and he gave us apples and bananas. We were so grateful. I wish I could see him again and say thank you. His help made us feel really great.

Some of my uncles came to Spokane before us. My uncles met us at the airport, and we stayed with them. We had some problems in the family, though. Some people in my family are Hindu, and some are Christian. They disagree with each other about religion and how to live. My grandparents moved to Ohio to be near other Nepali people they knew. I wanted to stay in Spokane and finish my schooling. One of my aunts was married to a Cuban man, and I moved in with them. I started to learn Spanish along with English. They had a cleaning business, and I helped them.

I started school at Ferris High School. The language was the hardest thing. I couldn't say anything, not even "hi" or "hello." I had never heard those words before. I thought, "If I don't reply, they will think I am a bad guy." I worried a lot about school.

At the Newcomer Center I learned English, and I started to understand more. I made really good friends from all over the world. Still, life was not easy. I still had no money, and I was very depressed sometimes. Sometimes I think some people are thinking, "He will not make it." But I always tell myself, "I will do something good in my life."

## Epilogue

I graduated from high school and started going to Eastern Washington University. Sometimes I take some time off of school to earn money to live. Also, I had to work to pay back

World Relief for my ticket to America. I have paid back everything I owed to World Relief now, and that feels really good.

When I have some money saved, I go back to school and study some more. I live alone and am doing my best to take care of myself. I am studying international affairs. I want to work for the United Nations someday. They helped me, because of the UN I am here, and I want to help other people.

Living with my grandparents in the refugee camp was not really fun. We were refugees, we had nothing, not even citizenship, but Nepal was my country, the place where I was born. Even though it was hard, I still love my country. I love living in the United States too. Living in the United States has given me so many opportunities to learn, to live, and to help other people.

I want to write a book about my life. There are a lot of people in the world who have bad experiences, like me. Sometimes they make bad choices, pick the wrong path. I hope that if I write a book, people can read it and be inspired to choose the right path. I want them to think, "He did it. Why not me too?"

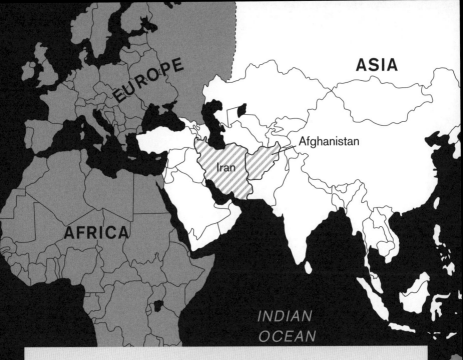

EUROPE

ASIA

Afghanistan

Iran

AFRICA

INDIAN
OCEAN

AUS

CHAPTER 9

# IRAN AND AFGHANISTAN

## A Few Facts about Iran

**AREA:** 628,872 square miles (1.63 million sq. km)

**POPULATION:** 83.9 million

**LANGUAGES:** Persian (Fārsī) and other Indo-Iranian languages

**RELIGIONS:** Islam, Christianity, Judaism, and Zoroastrianism

# A Few Facts about Afghanistan

**AREA:** 40,000 square miles (103,000 sq. km)

**POPULATION:** 37.5 million

**LANGUAGES:** Pashto, Persian (Dari), and other Indo-Iranian languages

**RELIGIONS:** Islam, with small groups practicing others

## A Little History

In ancient times, Iran was known as Persia. Ancient Persia was a multicultural and multilingual empire; a center of art, philosophy, and literature; and an important part of the Silk Road to the Far East. In the 600s, Arab Muslims conquered Iran and converted the country to Islam. Different Islamic groups fought for control, until eventually the majority of Iranians followed the Shia branch of Islam.

During the colonial age, foreign countries made trade agreements with Iran that benefited those countries more than the Iranian people. The United States and Europe worked to control the government of Iran. They helped overthrow elected government leaders and put people in power who would support policies that benefited American and European businesses and policies. Money from oil became an important part of the Iranian economy and increased the influence of foreign countries over the Iranian government. Literacy and access to health care increased, but government policies did not include freedom of speech, freedom of the press, or the right to vote. People who disagreed with the shah, Iran's leader, were arrested, tortured, and often never heard from again.

In 1979 the shah of Iran resigned. A religious leader named Ayatollah Khomeini took control of the Iranian government. The new government strictly enforced Islamic religious law. Although Ayatollah Khomeini died in 1989, the Iranian government remains authoritarian, with harsh punishments for speaking against the government.

## Why Did People Leave?

Religious minorities in Iran—including non-Muslims and non-Shia Muslims—faced persecution. So did Afghan refugees who crossed into Iran—first in the 1980s, during Russian and US military incursions into Afghanistan, and again after 2001, when the US launched another conflict in Afghanistan. Many Iranians viewed these refugees with suspicion. Afghanistan is mostly Sunni Islam, while Iran is mostly Shia. Iran's weak economy also meant that jobs were scarce for everyone. Facing discrimination and lack of opportunity, people left for other countries.

# Mortaza

**Afghanistan/Iran**
**US Entry: 2016**

My life story started in Iran. I was born in Iran to Afghani refugee parents. My parents had to leave Afghanistan because of the war there.

When I was ten years old, my parents, my little brother, my little sister, and I had to leave Iran because it was not safe for us. The Iranian government did not like Afghanis or Christians, and we were both. A lot of people died because of the government. Iranian people did not like refugees from Afghanistan. They called us "kafir," which is a bad word for stranger. My family and I escaped to Turkey. It is very strange: The Iranian government did not like us, they did not want us in their country, but still they did not want to let us leave.

My family and I went across the mountains to Turkey. My uncle said, "There are a lot of people in Turkey, in the city of Van, who will help us." So we moved to Van, Turkey. My uncle helped us, and the Catholic Church helped us. Turkey was a very different place for me and my family because people there use the Turkish language, and we only spoke Farsi. We had to learn Turkish. I could speak and read my language, but Turkish is very different. The letters for writing are different. Even the direction for writing is different. Turkish is written left to right like English, but Farsi is written right to left like Arabic.

We stayed in a refugee camp for two years. At the beginning, that first year, I didn't speak any Turkish. I was not happy. Because I could not speak any Turkish, I had no friends to hang out with. We went to the school to enroll us, my brother and me, but they would not enroll us in school. Then in 2011, Van had a big earthquake. It was a Saturday. I was outside when the ground under my feet started shaking. My parents and my siblings jumped out of the house. Everyone tried to move out into the street, but some people were stuck in their houses. Many houses crumbled. People were crying. It was a very rough day.

Before I went to sleep my mom told me, "If something starts happening, jump outside."

I told her, "I won't sleep. I cannot sleep, Mom." But when night came, I fell asleep. Around 11 p.m., the ground started shaking again, another earthquake, but this one was the strongest one. It was very strong, and capable of destroying half of the city.

This was painful because when the earthquake started, I had to jump outside, but I couldn't. I fell down on the rocks

In October 2011 Van, Turkey, had a very strong earthquake. Hundreds of people were killed, and thousands were made homeless.

and was injured. My mom and dad pulled me out of the house. I could not get any traction to walk because of my feet were numb. Fortunately, this did not last and I could walk.

We had to stay in the church for a few weeks, and my parents said, "This city it is not safe! We must move to a different city."

This new city did not work. We came back to Van after a few weeks. The UN sent us to live in a different city in Turkey, but we left that city too because of a different safety issue. Muslim people tried to hurt us. They hated people who were not Muslims.

Finally, we moved to the city of Mersin. Mersin is hot, dry, and near the sea. I lived in Mersin for six years. Mersin is one of Turkey's largest cities. I started to go to school and learned Turkish. We met new people and found a new church. Most of the people we met were Turkish, not Iranian. In Mersin the people were very kindhearted. Mersin soon seemed like my home.

I started to make friends and hung out with them. That made me happy. After I learned to speak Turkish and figured out the city, I started to think about working. So I started looking for a job. After I started looking for a job it took me two weeks to find a job. I started to work at a restaurant. I really didn't like my job, but I made a lot of friends and I started making money. Sometimes I worked as an interpreter too, between Farsi and Turkish. I shared my money with my family. I was working more than fifty hours a week.

Then we received the letter that said we were going to America. We were very happy and excited to be going to America. We had to wait another eleven months to go to America. We had to have interviews and medical exams.

Then it was time to go. We went to the bus station and bought tickets to go to Istanbul. It took fourteen hours on the bus to get to Istanbul. We spent the night in a hotel, and the next morning we went to the airport. They checked us and our luggage. We flew to Germany and then another plane to Chicago. Then we took another plane to Seattle, and finally to Spokane. We changed planes so many times.

Now I am eighteen. I live in the United States and I go to school to learn English and earn a high school diploma so I can go to university. I must start over again in the United States. In Turkey I had very good friends, but here I must make new friends. In Turkey I had a job, and in Spokane I have to find a new job. Moving to a new country is like starting a new life, like being a small child again.

## Epilogue

I graduated from high school in 2019. I had to take extra classes to graduate in three years. I had to graduate from high school before I was 21, or I would not be able to finish high school. I have had a job at Walmart for two years, but I am looking for a better job. With my job I help to support my family. I am going to university to study languages. Someday I want to be a professional translator. My family is very happy to be in the United States now.

# Nasrin

**Afghanistan/Iran**
**US Entry: 2015**

One sunny day in March 2000, I was born in Tehran, Iran. When I was born, my dad was living, but after two months, he died. My mom faced such hard days with my brothers and me.

My family and I are refugees from Afghanistan. My parents had to leave Afghanistan because of the war. They went to Iran. Life in Iran was hard for refugees from Afghanistan.

After my dad died, my mom started to work in a grocery store. She was so tired there, but she needed to work because my brothers and I were too small to work, and we all needed to eat.

At that time, life for my family and me was so hard. Our mom was so tired of being alone and she was unhappy.

After two years, my mom married with my father's brother. She married my uncle because this is a tradition in our culture when a woman's husband dies. They hoped to make a happy family. Together my mom and stepfather had three children. They were happy to have children, but they were not happy together.

My siblings and I did not like our stepfather. He was not a good husband and father. He did not come home, did not take care of his family. After a few years, my mother divorced him.

My mom's life became even harder. In Iran people did not like Afghan refugees. My mother was a single mother with seven children. We had to leave Iran. We decided to go to Turkey. By that time, I had five brothers and a sister.

Crossing to Turkey was not easy. We walked to Turkey through the mountains in the winter. That journey was so hard for me and for my family. We walked through the night without stopping—it was so cold. My legs were very tired and cold.

When we came to Turkey, my mom registered with the organization that helps refugees, UNHCR. She asked to go to Canada or the United States, someplace for a better life.

We started to live in Turkey. Turkish people were so friendly and good, and helpful with refugees, but the first days were hard because we did not speak Turkish. We needed to make money, because we did not have a home to sleep in, and we needed food to eat.

In Turkey I did not go to school in the beginning. The first year, my mom and I worked picking mushrooms. Every morning we woke up for work. The mushroom farm was cold and dark. That work was very hard for me. I did not like it there. I was ten years old.

After one year, my Turkish was better than before, and I started school. I was so happy because I wanted to talk with Turkish girls, and I wanted to know who they were. I wanted friends. School days were so great for me, but we could not live in Turkey for a long time. One day somebody called my mother, and they said, "You will go to the United States."

We had many interviews and medical checks. A year later, finally the UNHCR arranged for us to leave Turkey for America. We had lived in Turkey about four years.

We flew from Sivas, Turkey, to Los Angeles. It was such a long flight! We were very tired when we arrived in Los Angeles. We changed planes in Los Angeles and flew to Spokane.

A man from World Relief came to the airport with a big van to take us and our luggage to my mother's friend's house.

Those first days, we children were so scared of America. We did not really understand anything about American culture. We did not speak English. Everything was different.

My older brothers and I started school in Ferris High School. The first school days were boring because we did not understand anything, but soon everything began to change. We started to understand.

Now we live in the United States, in Spokane, Washington. Now Spokane is home, and I want to forget the bad times in my life. I am happy here.

## Epilogue

In June 2019 I graduated from Ferris High School. Now I go to college to prepare for a career. Here in America I have so many choices, so many opportunities, it is hard to decide on a career! I want a career where I can help other people and my family.

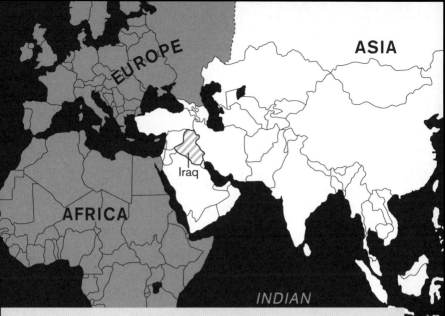

EUROPE

ASIA

AFRICA

INDIAN

Iraq

## CHAPTER 10
# IRAQ

......................................................

### A Few Facts about Iraq

**AREA:** 167,618 square miles (434,128 sq. km)

**POPULATION:** 39.79 million

**LANGUAGES:** Arabic, Kurdish, Turkoman Assyrian/Neo-Aramaic, and
Armenian

**RELIGIONS:** Islam, with small groups practicing Christianity, Judaism,
and Zoroastrianism

### A Little History

Archaeologists tell us that the land we now call Iraq is the
birthplace of human civilization. The region where people
first built towns and cities, and where the empires of the ancient
Sumerians, Babylonians, and Assyrians all developed, includes

modern-day Iraq, Iran, Turkey, and Syria. At different times in history, the ancient Greeks, Romans, and Persians each ruled what is now Iraq. Around 750 CE, the region was controlled by Persia and converted to Islam. Baghdad became an important center of Islamic learning.

In 1968 the Ba'ath political party took control of Iraq. The goal of the Ba'ath Party was to unite the Arab countries in the Middle East through socialism. Under the rule of the Ba'ath Party, Iraq's economy was strong, and Iraq was well respected in the Arab world, but civil liberties such as freedom of speech were limited.

Saddam Hussein became the president of Iraq in 1979. Under Saddam's rule, Iraq invaded Iran in 1980. The Iran-Iraq War lasted almost eight years.

In August 1990, Iraq invaded Kuwait, starting the First Gulf War and drawing condemnation from the United Nations, the United States, Britain, and many Arab countries. The United States led a coalition of countries to fight Iraq. The war ended in victory for the coalition in February of 1991.

After the First Gulf War, Iraq was forced to destroy its chemical weapons and stop building nuclear weapons. Other nations agreed not to buy Iraqi oil until Iraq cooperated with weapons inspections. The loss of oil money through this embargo was very hard on the Iraqi economy.

On September 11, 2001, nineteen terrorists hijacked planes and flew them into the World Trade Center in New York; the Pentagon near Washington, DC; and a cornfield in Pennsylvania. Almost three thousand people died. None of the terrorists were from Iraq, but the United States considered Iraq a sponsor of terrorism. In 2003 the United States, with the help of Britain, began a second war with Iraq. Saddam was eventually arrested, and put on trial for crimes against humanity.

He was found guilty and executed by the new, US-supported Iraqi government in 2006.

Officially, all faiths were equal in Iraq. However, friction between Shia Muslims and Sunni Muslims in Iraq led to civil war after the fall of Saddam. Terrorist organizations formed. Life in Iraq became very difficult. The country was severely damaged by war, and the economy was weak, making jobs and necessities scarce.

## Why Did People Leave?

Many Iraqis who helped the US military—for example, by working as interpreters—were targeted by other Iraqis who did not want the United States in Iraq. They received death threats, and those who could get out of the country left. Religious violence was another reason for people to leave. Different Islamic groups began to fight for control of the country. Some people used the ongoing fighting as a cover for criminal activity: stealing, kidnapping, and terrorizing. Fearing for their lives, people left for Jordan, Syria, or Turkey.

# Antonius

**Iraq**
**US Entry: 2009**

Before the war, my life in Bagdad was normal. I lived in a big, beautiful house with a front garden and a back garden. We had orange trees, apple trees, and flowers. Our fence was covered with gardenias. It was beautiful.

On school days, I would get up and walk the two blocks to school with my friends. After second period we had a fifteen-minute recess. My friends and I played games like tic-tac-toe or hopscotch.

After school, before we even changed out of our school uniforms, we would bring out the soccer ball and gather all the cool kids on the block to play soccer on the street. We played until my mother came home from her job at the bank around 3 pm. Then it was time for a shower and lunch. We ate five times a day, so our lunch was a little bit later and our dinner was around 9 pm. Then I started my homework. Around 6 pm my friends and I would gather for another round of games and then dinner and then bed.

Sometimes if I slacked and did not do my homework, I would get hit on the palms of my hand with a stick. Teachers could be very severe in Iraq! My life did not have many worries, as long as I did my homework.

I was an eleven-year-old when the war started. At first life was pretty much the same for me. The fighting was not in Baghdad; it was in places like Fallujah and Mosul that still supported Saddam Hussein. In Baghdad the Americans were heroes. People were happy.

Then the civil war began. Sunni terrorists blew up the Al-Askari Shrine in Samarra, which is a very important holy site for the Shia Muslims. Then there was retaliation. Shia would go into Sunni mosques, burn them, and kill everyone inside. Terrorists would set off bombs. The government could not control anything. So many people died—thousands died on both sides. All of that led to ISIS.

Religious persecution and safety became concerns because my family is Christian. The school day was shortened due to security concerns. Church time was also shortened. Mass used to take two to three hours but was cut to 1half that.

Islamic extremist groups began targeting Christians. When a Danish cartoonist made a drawing of Muhammad, large numbers of people went out into the street demonstrating against Christians. [Islam forbids depictions of the Prophet Muhammad.] Extremists started vandalizing our churches.

We tried to live our lives like normal, go to school, play soccer with friends, but much of my life after the war began was very dark. My mother had a new job in the Green Zone, the American-controlled part of the city. Everyone working for the Americans became a target. The workers would ride a bus. They would get dropped off at a different place every day, so terrorists could not plan an attack. My mother would call to tell me where she was dropped off, and I would drive the car to go get her. I would worry that someone would follow me, that I was a target. The driving age in Iraq was eighteen, and I was only thirteen, but it was okay. We were in a war—who was going to complain about underage driving?

The last year I spent in Iraq before we moved out of the country was hard. It became normal to be sitting, drinking tea, and hear gunshots and explosions close by. I lost some of my friends to the civil war between Sunnis and Shias. My neighbor Noor was kidnapped but thankfully was let go for a ransom.

Here and there were a few beautiful moments. The last happy moment I remember was my cousin's birth in 2005. I remember being in the hospital with my mother and the whole family waiting while my uncle's wife was delivering. It was a happy moment to have a new family member. We baptized her in the following month. She has brought joy to the family ever since.

In 2007, when I was fifteen years old, my entire family decided to leave Iraq. Our last days in our country were a mess. Not only was my family leaving, but many of my neighbors were also leaving the country. My family was panicking [and trying] to get the passports ready and gather some of our belongings. There were restrictions on how much money we could take with us. How would we live without money? My grandparents and my aunt's and uncle's families left Iraq two weeks before us.

My mother, my two older brothers, and I followed them. It was a long ride to Damascus, Syria. In Syria we filed as refugees to come to the United States.

We spent two years in Damascus waiting for our immigration case to be processed. Our lives were on hold, just waiting. The four of us lived in a very, very small, two-bedroom apartment, about the size of our living room in Baghdad. Each day I woke up wondering why. Why did I even bother to wake up? We had to keep thinking, "It will get better."

In Syria I did not go to school. I worked in a clothing shop fourteen hours a day, seven days a week—Christmas, Easter, every day. We all worked. Finally, in July 2009, we received our travel date to America.

The journey to America was very long and stressful.

Along the way we had help from the International Organization for Migration. The IOM crew waited for us at the gate in Paris, took us to the next gate, and asked us to wait for our flight. We stopped in Paris for six hours. Our next stop was JFK airport in New York. We were helped by another group, with an Egypt man who spoke Arabic with us.

We were gathered in a waiting room for our biometrics processing and finally spent the night at a bad motel rented by the group that was helping us with the moving process. Early in the morning we went back to JFK and headed to Chicago. There we waited for a few hours, and I was hungry, so my mom gave me a $100 bill to go get us some food. I did not know American money yet, and I did not speak English yet. I went to McDonald's and didn't know how to order. I stood in line and watched how other people ordered. I saw the numbers and pictures on the menu, and I raised my hand gesturing the No. 5 meal. They gave me a No. 5 meal. When I went back to my mother and brothers, they asked, "Where is our food?" I told them they would have to go and get theirs.

Finally, we boarded our final flight to Spokane. We arrived hungry and tired and full of uncertainty. We did not know what was ahead of us in this completely different world. We spoke a little bit of English, which helped us a bit.

We did not really know what America would be like. We had only seen America through the lenses of Hollywood before we came here. Imagine the shock we had when we were landing at the Spokane International Airport! It was the opposite of "wow." I felt like an abandoned dog on an old country road! Now I love Spokane, I wouldn't move anywhere else, but then Spokane seemed like such a small town.

World Relief had an apartment ready for us. After the tiny apartment in Syria, it was comfortable. My oldest brother and

I went on a walk around our new neighborhood to explore the area. A person from World Relief came and helped us get our paperwork done. I remember waiting in line to get our social security numbers and get our work authorization cards. We also did some biometrics. I remember many trips to the clinic to get all our vaccinations.

My first day in high school I was terrified. How could I make it with no English?

In my first class I sat down by a tall skinny Russian guy and realized I was not alone. There were other newcomers learning English. We had classes for learning English.

I didn't know how to get home, so my teacher printed me a Google map and explained how to find my house. It was an

Biometrics are biological and physical metrics that are used for identification, including finger prints, retina scans, and facial recognition.

adventure. I made it home, and I made it back to school. My life was no longer on hold; I was living again.

In the beginning life was hard, but it was fun as well. Americans are good people and we received so much help along the way. Our second week in the US, someone knocked on our door. We opened it and saw a tall gentleman and two young ladies. They introduced themselves as Brent, Amy, and Sarah. They were from Global Neighborhood. Sarah volunteered to help us with whatever we needed. She has been our friend ever since. She came in once a week to check on us and see what we needed. She did it in way that made us feel like friends. She helped us with our taxes. She took us to Seattle for the first time, and she taught us so much about navigating our way in society. We met many great people along the way.

Everything we did was an adventure during our first few months. Asking for directions seemed like a final exam. I was nervous, and I practiced the sentences many times in my head before I asked someone. Learning English was exciting, as was finding places to shop for quality clothes, quality food, and other things. When we came it was during the recession, so it was difficult for my family to find jobs, but we managed. Simply being here was exciting!

Everything was confusing in the first days: taxes, language, school, paperwork, job applications. But things started making sense fairly quickly, with the help of many friends. We could not have done it without having great American friends, genuinely good people who never asked for anything in return.

## Epilogue

In 2018 I graduated from Whitworth University with a double major: physics and math. I considered graduate school, but I chose to go back to Panda Express, where I had worked while I was in school. They rehired me as a manager right away, and the pay is good. Plus, I enjoy moving around rather than sitting at a desk.

My dream is to build a family. Not in the near future, but maybe in five years, I'll get married and have kids. My mother wants to be a grandmother. For now, I'm focusing on my career. Owning my own house is my near-future, top-priority goal.

# Zahraa

**Iraq**
**US Entry: 2013**

Can you image being thirteen years old and having your parents tell you to get ready to move from your homeland to a completely new world? This is my story. I was this child whose parents said, "Get ready to move." This is the situation that forced me to start to grow up and become more mature and responsible.

When I was born in Baghdad in 1998, and for a few years after, my life was good. I was surrounded by my cousins and my big family. I was the only sister to three loving brothers. My country was very beautiful and very safe. My family had a beautiful house with a garden and large yard, and I was able to go wherever I wanted to go. But when I was old enough to get ready to go to school, my country became unsafe, and we started hearing about bad things happening. Every day and every night, we heard planes and bombs and the sounds of guns. People were killing other people; no place was safe. It was horrible. I started worrying about my homeland and my lovely family. I did not know it then, but my childhood was coming to an end.

When I was nine years old, due to the dangerous situation in Iraq, my parents decided to move us from Iraq to Turkey, to be safe. Leaving all my family behind in Iraq was a very sad time for me. The last night, my family gathered together in our home to say goodbye. My grandparents, uncles, aunts, and cousins stayed together that whole night. The next day we started our journey on a bus crowded with strangers, with only the things we could carry in a suitcase. The rest of our family decided they could not leave Iraq. I did not even understand what was happening. I was so afraid. The trip to Turkey took three days. Our bus had a police escort until we were out of Iraq.

In Turkey, we stayed with a friend of my father's for a few weeks while my father looked for a place for us to live. Finally, he found an apartment in the city of Bolu, Turkey. It was not as nice as our home, but now the situation was different, and we were happy to just be safe. My life was better because I was safer, but it was hard because I did not know any Turkish, nor did I know any people.

My family registered in the refugee program as soon as we could. In Turkey I felt like my life was on hold, waiting for something to happen, and not knowing when that would happen. I felt unsettled because I did not know how long I would live in Turkey, and I did not know what country I would go to in the refugee program. I just wanted to be somewhere safe. My uncle lived in the USA, and we hoped that we could go to live near him, but we did not know for sure if that was possible, or how long it might take.

My childhood ended quickly, and I was forced to grow up, even if I did not want to. I had to adapt to everything that was new. I had to learn that life goes on and never will stop for anyone. I could no longer play with my cousins and be carefree. Now I had more responsibilities, like taking care of my young brothers. Also, I had the biggest responsibility when I was interacting with Turkish people: I had to learn the Turkish language. I had to be serious, know how to act, and how to talk in the right way with others.

In Iraq I was in fifth grade, and in Turkey I was put in fifth grade again. I was just wanting the language. I knew we would not be staying in Turkey, but still I began to make friends with other refugee children and Turkish children. Everyone was very friendly, and I learned more language from my friends than from my teachers. My life started to be almost normal.

Finally, three years, my family got approved to move to the United States, to Spokane, Washington, from our refugee home in Turkey. My parents had gone through many interviews and we had medical checks and lots of shots. I hated the shots and cried. My family and I started packing up and buying new clothes to take with us. As we prepared to leave, we wanted to make great memories and took lots of pictures to remember where we came from. I realized I had made so many friends, and I was sad to leave, and afraid to start over again. I knew that I would have to start from the beginning again with no language and no friends. Still, I was very happy that my real life was going to begin again after those years and months of waiting on hold.

In June 2013, on a Thursday afternoon, I boarded a plane from Turkey to Los Angeles. Then we transferred to a plane to Seattle, then another plane to Spokane, Washington. It was a very difficult trip for me because that was the first time I had ever been on an airplane, and I was not traveling for fun. Instead, it was the trip that was going to change my life completely. I was full of worries and fears. When we changed planes, I was very afraid I would not catch my airplane and I would be stranded in a foreign county. I was afraid that I would never land in American and find my new home. I was afraid I would never get into my new school and get my education.

When I arrived in Spokane, when I saw my uncle waiting for us in the airport to take us to his house, I felt much better. I remember it was dark and raining outside. My parents, my brothers, and I spent twenty days at my uncle's house while World Relief found us a house of our own.

Soon school started. World Relief took me and my siblings to the school's registration office. I expected to be in middle school. I had only finished seventh grade in Turkey, but they put me in ninth grade, and right then I felt that I had grown up because now I was a high school student. This was the education that I could not have in my country, and now I would have it. I was super happy that I was going to be one of the people who could have their dreams come true, but at the same time I was sad and fearful of the language that was going to be in my way and not let me be successful.

Soon I arrived at Ferris High School. I started at the Newcomer Center, level one. With the passing of the days I learned the language, just like I learned Turkish. Now I am a senior at Ferris High School and adept with the language, with everything. I am super excited that I am going to graduate in less than three months.

## Epilogue

Now I have graduated from high school and I attend university. I am a citizen of the USA, and have my American passport—that it is an amazing feeling. Everyone in my family are citizens of the United States now. We came here not knowing anyone, and not even knowing the language. Now we speak English, and my parents have jobs. We had hard times, but we have good lives now. My older brother and I are studying and working.

I am studying political science and communications at Eastern Washington University. In the future I hope to have a career working with an agency like the UNHCR, which helped my family and me when we were refugees. I want to help with translating or process refugees or work in governmental law. Someday I hope to be married with two children and my own

The hijab is a type of hair covering.

home. I hope to be able to travel back and forth between Turkey and the USA, but I do not want to go back to Iraq. I do not have good memories of Iraq, just fear. I had no opportunities, no future there, just hiding and worrying.

Coming to the USA was the beginning of my life, my door to opportunity to be what I am supposed to be. The people at my high school, Ferris, were kind to me. Even though I wear the hijab, people were always respectful. No one was mean, no one was asking, "Why are you here?" "Why do you wear that on your head?" I like my life here in the USA. I have opportunity here. I have knowledge here.

ASIA

EUROPE

TIC
N

Syria

AFRICA

INDIAN

CHAPTER II

# SYRIA

...............................................................

## A Few Facts about Syria

**AREA:** 71,498 square miles (185,180 sq. km)
**POPULATION:** 20.4 million
**LANGUAGES:** Arabic, Kurdish, Armenian, and Aramaic
**RELIGIONS:** Islam and Christianity

## A Little History

People have been living in the area now known as Syria, Iraq, and Iran for thousands of years. In ancient times the eastern side of the Mediterranean Sea was all called Syria. At different times in history this region was controlled by the Greeks, Romans, and Persians. Syria was part of the Byzantine Empire until 637 CE, when Muslim armies defeated the Byzantine Empire.

Damascus, the capital of Syria, became the capital of the Islamic Empire, which spread Islamic rule west across North Africa to Spain and east to northern India.

In the 1500s the Ottoman Empire conquered Syria. After World War I (1914–1918), the Ottoman Empire was broken up and the League of Nations gave France control over Syria and Lebanon.

Syrians wanted their own government, so many rebellions broke out. In 1936 France agreed to work toward independence for Syria, but kept military and economic control over Syria. France remained in Syria in some form until after World War II, when Britain forced France to evacuate their troops. In 1946 Syria finally became a completely independent country. Then, in 1947, the Arab Socialist Ba'ath Party was formed in Syria. The Ba'athists wanted all the Arab countries to be independent from European control.

Like many newly independent nations after World War II, Syria's government was unstable, with different factions fighting for control.

Hafiz al-Assad became the leader of Syria in 1970 by overthrowing the president and putting his rivals in prison. Assad focused on building up a strong military. He involved Syria in many conflicts with other countries. His authoritarian government controlled the press and denied people free speech. Hafiz al-Assad was the leader of Syria until his death in 2000, when his son Bashar al-Assad succeeded him.

Bashar al-Assad strengthened Syria's economy but continued his father's authoritarian style of government. People who disagreed with the government were often thrown in prison. In 2011 the pro-democracy movement known as the Arab Spring came to Syria, sparking the Syrian Civil War. Pro-democracy rebels, called the Free Syrian Army, fought Assad's Syrian Army.

A terrorist organization known as the Islamic State of Iraq and Syria (ISIS) joined the fighting against the Syrian military and took control of parts of the country. ISIS committed numerous acts of violence, from executions to the destruction of historical sites. To complicate the situation even more, the US military supported the rebels and fought against ISIS; Russia supported Assad's army against the rebels but also fought ISIS. Syrians faced war on all sides.

## Why Did People Leave?

Syria's civil war endangered civilians all over the country. Some people tried to make their way to Europe; some went to Jordan; others went to Turkey. Jordan and Turkey did not have enough room or jobs for so many refugees. With the help of UNHCR, many Syrians applied for resettlement to other countries.

# Neroz

Syria
US Entry: 2016

My family are Kurdish people. I am from Syria. That was my home when I was a baby. I speak Arabic. There are six people in my family: me, my brother, my two little sisters, my mom, and my dad. My brother, one of my sisters, and I are deaf. We were born mostly deaf; we could only hear a little. Our parents can hear, though.

Before the war, our life was happy. I went to school. I had friends. We visited my uncle who had a farm and raised sheep.

In 2011, the war began. The war destroyed houses and buildings. There was fighting, shooting, and bombs. At night we could not sleep because of the bombs and guns. The noises were so loud. The war made my brother completely deaf. Many people died. My little cousin was killed. My family had to go or die. Life matters most. Everything we do starts with being alive. We went to Turkey so we could live.

My family moved to Turkey in 2015. My whole family moved from Syria to Turkey. We traveled there by bus.

My little sisters went to school in Turkey, but my brother and I could not. In Syria I went to school. I liked school. In Turkey, my brother and I worked. I was fifteen years old. My brother was thirteen years old. He worked in a clothing cleaner shop with my dad. They cleaned and folded clothes. They got paid $10 every day they worked. They worked with many bosses and with many clothes.

I worked in a factory making paper bags. I used the money I earned to help my family. I was in charge of buying drinking water for my family. The water in the house was only good for washing. Water for drinking was expensive.

My mom made dolma, stuffed grape leaves, which is still my favorite food. I am learning to make them myself.

Turkey became my home for one year. I made friends in Turkey, but we could not stay in Turkey. We are Syrian and we are Kurdish, so we had to apply to be refugees so we could go to another country to live. The officials had to stamp and sign our papers, and it took a very long time. We had many interviews and doctor appointments. Finally, we were given our papers to travel to America.

The day came to leave Turkey. We packed our bags, sat, and waited a long time. We took a bus to the airport. Finally, we got on the airplane, and my whole family flew to America. It was my first time on an airplane. We flew for a long time. I was excited and nervous. People we met talked different languages.

My father's friends met us in Spokane and drove us to their home. I looked around. It was a beautiful home. Everything was beautiful and peaceful. We unpacked.

Spokane was very hot when we arrived. In Turkey I had to wear a hijab. In Spokane, I took a picture of me in my hijab. Then I stopped wearing it.

We had a new home. I went right to school. The school looked beautiful. The teacher was nervous. She never had deaf students before. My brother and I were her first deaf students. We began to learn American Sign Language and English. My parents took American Sign Language and English classes too. In Syria and Turkey, we used "home signs" instead. I had a hearing aid and I could hear a little and read lips. Now, my brother, my sister, and I have cochlear implants. We are learning to hear and speak. We have speech therapy every week.

I felt happy when I came to Spokane. I was happy finally to be with friends. I miss Syria and Turkey, but I like Spokane. I have friends and I go to school in Spokane. When I graduate from high school, I want to go to Gallaudet University in Washington, D.C. Then I will decide on a career. My brother wants to become a mechanic and fix cars.

ARCTIC OCEAN

EASTERN
EUROPE

ASIA

ATLANTIC
OCEAN

AFRICA

PAC
OC

PART 3

# EASTERN EUROPE

E astern Europe includes the European countries east of Germany, Austria, and Italy and west of the Caucasus Mountains, the Ural Mountains, and the Ural River. This includes several countries once controlled by the Union of Soviet Socialist Republics (USSR) and the eastern portion of Russia.

AREA: approximately 8.65 million square miles (22.4 million sq. km)

POPULATION: approximately 292.74 million

COUNTRIES: 7 countries and 3 republics, but often as many as 23 countries depending on how you draw the borders

LANGUAGES: over 100

RELIGIONS: Christianity, Islam, Buddhism, Judaism, and others

Russia

ASIA

EUROPE

# CHAPTER 12
# RUSSIA

## A Few Facts about Russia

**AREA:** 6.6 million square miles (17.1 million sq. km)

**POPULATION:** 147 million

**LANGUAGES:** Russian, Tatar, Chechen, and over 100 others

**RELIGIONS:** Christianity and Islam

## A Little History

Most citizens of Russia are ethnic Russians living in European Russia, but Russia is very diverse, with more than 150 different ethnic groups.

From the 1400s to 1917, Russia was a monarchy led by a tsar, or king. The Russian Empire had a feudal system of land ownership and labor until 1861. Serfs, or peasants, could not own land but had to stay on the land where they were born and work for the landowner. The landowners had complete control over serfs. Even after the end of the feudal system, Russians had few rights.

In 1917 the Russian people rebelled and overthrew the tsarist government. Eventually, the government was taken over by the Communists under the leadership of Vladimir Lenin. Over the next few years, Communists fought against anti-Communists in a civil war. The Communists prevailed.

In 1922 Russia formed the Union of Soviet Socialist Republics (USSR) with four other republics. In the Cyrillic alphabet this is CCCP, which is pronounced "es-es-es-air." The word *soviet* (совет in Cyrillic) means "a council or group that gives advice to the leader." Eventually the USSR grew to include fifteen republics.

When Lenin died in 1924, Joseph Stalin took over leadership of the USSR. Under Stalin, the government took complete control over farms and businesses. Millions of Soviet citizens who disagreed with Stalin's policies were killed or sent to prisons and work camps. Civil rights were limited, and Soviet citizens were not allowed to travel out of the USSR without government approval. Under the USSR's constitution, people had religious freedom, but in reality, practicing religion was strongly discouraged and even persecuted.

In the 1980s, a new policy of glasnost, the Russian word for openness, allowed more freedom of expression. In 1989 Soviet citizens began to protest against Communist governments and declare independence from the USSR. On December 26, 1991, the USSR officially dissolved, and Russia became an independent country again.

# Why Do People Leave?

In the former USSR, people can openly practice the Russian Orthodox branch of Christianity after decades of religious suppression, but other faiths still face persecution. Once the government allowed emigration, evangelical Christians began leaving Russia as religious refugees, seeking religious freedom in the West.

# Vika

**Russia**
**US Entry: 1997**

My name is Viktoria; my friends call me Vika. I was born in Russia in the city of Krasnoyarsk, Siberia. In Russia, I lived in a big apartment building. Right now, other people live there.

I came to America in March 1997. I like to live in America.

Russia is very different from the USA. In Russia, where I lived, we had different houses, cars, and other things. For example, American people do not have big gardens. Americans have grass lawns. In Russia, people have big gardens. Russia does not have big stores like in America; Russia has many smallshops.

Russia is the biggest country in the world. There are a lot of forests, fields, mountains, rivers, seas, lakes, and etc. The nature is very beautiful, especially in the countryside. A lot of people of different nations live there.

The capital city of Russia is Moscow. This city is very old. The biggest rivers in Russia are the Ob and the Lena. The biggest lake is Lake Baikal. In Russia people go camping and hiking in the Ural Mountains. They go to Lake Baikal and swim or water ski.

The Russian flag is red, white, and blue like the American flag, but it just has one stripe of each color. A few years ago, there was another flag. That other flag was red, with a gold star, and a hammer and sickle.

My school in Russia had two floors and three buildings.

Thirty students were in my class. We had to wear uniforms until fourth grade.

In Russia the language is different. In my first class we learned letters like this:

а б в г д е з и й к л м н о п р с т у ф х ц ь ы ю я

These are some of the 33 letters I learned in my first class.

Russian schools did not have school buses like in America. Russian students have to walk to school or ride a city bus and pay for tickets. I walked to school because I lived very close to my school. From my bedroom window, I could see into my classroom. I could see my teacher at her desk. I loved being so close to my school. I loved school.

I would wake up every morning, eat breakfast, and run to school just as the bell was ringing. We had so many students that the school was in two shifts. I went to school in the morning, and then I would go home at about 2 p.m. My younger brother prepared my lunch because he had afternoon school, and our parents worked. Then my brother would go to school for the afternoon shift, and later I would prepare dinner for him. With our parents working, we were alone a lot of the time.

After I ate my lunch, I would run outside to play with my friends. My friends and I, maybe fifteen kids, stayed together like a family of children. We would take off and play, have adventures, go hiking, go to a lake, find an abandoned orchard and eat apples. Parents never worried about where we were; they trusted us to be together and take care of each other.

In winter I would put on my skates and skate for hours. In Siberia the sun goes down so early in the winter that it was easy to forget what time it was, and in the summer the sun stayed up so long that we did not think about how late it was. We had a lot of fun times.

When I was young, it did not matter to anyone that my family was Christian. Later, when we were old enough to notice these things, sometimes our friends would make bad jokes about us going to church. There was some bullying. At that time the country was changing.

In middle school, my homeroom teacher would ask me stay after school a couple of times a week and talk to me about religion, ask me questions to make me doubt my religion, basically try to brainwash me. I did not mention it to my parents for a couple of months. I thought, "I can take it, I am not scared." Then she was pushing so much that I was kind of scared of her. Then I talked to my parents. They came to school and put an end to it. My brother and I did not have troublesome experiences about religion like our grandparents or parents had when they were children.

My grandmother, my mother's mother, lived with us, but the rest of my mother's family had been in the United States for a long time. They wanted us to come to the USA to reunite the family. The Soviet Union was breaking apart, things were changing, and everything got very messy. My parents decided to join the family in the USA.

We had to decide what to leave and what to bring.

I had a pair of roller skates from Germany someone had given to me as a present. They were pretty heavy, with lots of metal parts, and my parents told me, "You cannot bring the roller skates. They are too big and too heavy."

But I said, "I am going to take them to America! No matter what, I am taking them with me!" I put them in a backpack and put them on my back and carried them. I did not take a lot of treasures to America, but I took my roller skates.

What I could not take with me were my friends. I did not want to go to America and leave my school and my friends. It was a nightmare for me. I even told my parents that I would not go anywhere, they should leave me in Russia. Of course, they were not going to do that! I was only fourteen. At that time, I was singing in the church choir, and I loved it. One of my cousins in America told me that in America there were choir classes in school. I knew that if I came to America, I could take this class. That choir class became my light at the end of the tunnel.

We did not tell our friends and neighbors that we were going to America. Even many of my father's relatives did not know that we were moving to America. At that time there was a lot of jealousy. It was very scary to let people know that you were moving out of the country. People knew if you were moving, it meant you sold some things and you would have a lot of money. If people knew we were leaving they might come to steal from us and maybe even kill us. We could not have a goodbye party. We could not say goodbye to anyone.

We had to sell our apartment. My parents asked the people who were buying the apartment if we could stay until the end of the month, and they said, "Yes, no problem." When all the papers were signed, they said, "Now you have to get out of here."

We were still packing, still selling things we could not take with us. We had to hurry, pack everything, and go. We gave away many valuable things because we did not have time to sell them.

My parents, my grandmother, my brother, and I traveled from Krasnoyarsk to Moscow with all of our big bags. Our family in America told us, "In America they do not have normal pillows! We cannot get good blankets and pillows. You must bring pillows and blankets." This was because in Russia pillows are square, but in America most pillows are rectangular.

Blankets in America are not made of wool or filled with feathers like Russian blankets. So we had big bags with pillows and blankets, plus everything else we were taking to America.

In Moscow we got lost on the subway. My father said, "Stay right here. I will go find out where we need to go."

There we were with our big pile of bags in the subway station that was very crowded with people. We had to watch carefully so no one would steal any of our bags. So my mother moved us a little to the side, out of that crowded place. When my father came back, he could not see us. He was running up and down looking for us. Finally, he found us, and he said, "Why did you move? I have been looking for you! Now we are going to be late!" Fortunately, we made it to the airport on time.

On the plane everything was fine. Grandmother was trying to learn English. My brother and I had studied English in school, so we knew a little bit of English. She would say, "Teach me how to say *Give me some juice, please* and *I need to go to the bathroom*." Of course, she would say it in some funny way, and we all laughed. We were not thinking about where we were going, we were just having fun.

The flight over the ocean was very long, and the plane was playing the movie *Titanic*. With all the water below us, and the bumps and turbulence, we were watching *Titanic*.

I barely remember landing in New York and changing planes. We were so tired. Finally, we were in Spokane. A big crowd of relatives and church people met us in the airport with balloons and flowers. It was a very happy arrival. Our relatives had rented an apartment for us and put food in the cupboards and refrigerator.

We had many appointments for shots, checkups, fingerprints, and papers. We had to open the map and find our way.

We were always late to our appointments because we had to find our way on busses. Our relatives had their own lives, and they had jobs; they could not take us to appointments.

We arrived in Spokane in March, and someone said, "It is so close to the end of the school year, you probably will not go to school until September." My brother and I were thinking, *This is so good!* We were so happy with this idea of a long vacation. Then someone said, "Okay, it is time for you to start school."

I said, "What? I am not going to school until September." But we had to start school.

Our church was sponsoring another family. Their daughter, Olga, was my age. We became best friends. We went to school together.

Our first day of school was very strange. Many of the students were dressed in black and wearing strange white masks. Olga and I did not know it, but this day was a drug awareness day, and some people were dressed like this to show how many people each day die from drugs. They looked very strange and scary. We wondered if our teacher would look like this.

Somehow we found our way to our English class. We slowly peeked into the classroom, and the teacher asked, "Are you Olga and Vika?"

"Yes."

"Come in."

We met our teacher and began to learn English. I had choir class; it was like heaven. I was happy to be in America.

## Epilogue

I graduated from high school and went to the community college. Then I transferred to Eastern Washington University and studied education so I could be a teacher. I got married and had three children. I plan to go back to university to study to be a language pathologist, or speech therapist.

Olga and I are still best friends. I named my daughter Olga after her.

I was always very social, but Olga was shy, and one of her feet was not straight. When we were still in school, I decided to teach Olga to roller skate. She said she could not do it, but I told her, "You can do it. I will prove it to you." I made her try. She wore my German roller skates that I had brought in my backpack from Siberia. I held her hand and she skated, until finally she could skate by herself. I told her, "You see, you did it. You can do it. You just have to try." I have no regrets about carrying those heavy German roller skates all the way from Siberia to Spokane; they helped Olga develop her confidence.

I would like to go to visit Russia again. My daughter is a ballerina, and someday she would like to see the Bolshoi Ballet. My roots are in Russia, in Russian poetry and music and nature. I tell my children these are their roots too. My family was sent to Siberia three generations ago by the Tsar, and Siberia is part of us now. I know that if I go back everything will be different, though. America is part of us now too, and I am happy that I came here.

CHAPTER 13

# UKRAINE

......................................................................

## A Few Facts about Ukraine

**AREA:** 233,032 square miles (603,549 sq. km)

**POPULATION:** 44.24 million

**LANGUAGES:** Ukrainian, Russian, and several others

**RELIGIONS:** Christianity, Judaism, and other religions

## A Little History

The rich farmland of Ukraine has always made it desirable. Slavic people have lived in what is now Ukraine since before the Common Era. The Mongol Empire ruled Ukraine and much of the surrounding area from the 1200s to the mid-1400s, when the Mongols gave control of the Crimean

Peninsula to the Ottoman Empire. During this time, Poland and Lithuania fought the Mongols, with Poland claiming parts of Ukraine and Lithuania claiming other parts.

Ukrainians under Polish control started a revolution against Poland in 1648. This conflict weakened Poland, and other countries invaded Ukraine. By the early nineteenth century, control was officially split between the Russian Empire and the Austro-Hungarian Empire. Although their country no longer existed as a nation, the Ukrainian people maintained their language and cultural identity. The Russian government was afraid that the Ukrainians would rebel and demand independence, so they banned the study of Ukrainian language and literature in schools.

At the end of World War I, when the Austro-Hungarian Empire collapsed, Ukrainians declared independence. But Ukraine was absorbed into the USSR as one of its original four republics in 1922.

Stalin's collectivization policies were devastating to Ukrainians. In 1932 to 1933, so much grain was taken from Ukraine to feed the rest of the USSR that a terrible famine killed many Ukrainians. Many Ukrainian writers, artists, and intellectuals were arrested. With so many Ukrainians dead or in prison, people struggled to maintain Ukrainian education, culture, and language.

After Stalin's death in 1953, the USSR's anti-Ukrainian policies ended. Ownership of the Crimean Peninsula was transferred back to Ukraine in 1954. Many of the people who had been imprisoned in Russia were allowed to return to Ukraine. However, Ukraine's natural resources were still important to the USSR, and the beaches along the Black Sea and the Crimean Peninsula were favorite vacation spots. The government continued to work to make Ukraine more Russian and less Ukrainian.

In 1989 Ukrainian activists called for independence from the USSR and an end to communism. The country voted overwhelmingly for independence and officially became an independent nation in December 1991.

## Why Do People Leave?

Even after communism ended in Ukraine, many people with strong religious beliefs chose to leave Ukraine as refugees. In 2014 eastern Ukraine became unsafe for civilians when Russia invaded and annexed the Crimean Peninsula, reclaiming the land that had been returned to Ukraine in 1954. The ensuing conflict between Russia and Ukraine displaced over one hundred thousand people, and more than three million people are in need of humanitarian aid.

# Irina

**Ukraine**
**US Entry: 1998**

I was born in Krivoy Rog, Ukraine, in the USSR. My life in Ukraine was a normal life. I had a big, happy, loving family. My mother worked in an office, and my father worked in a mine. We lived in the city, near our relatives, except one uncle who had emigrated to America in the 1980s.

Our uncle who lived in the United States applied for a visa for my family to go to America too. The visa required us to go to Israel first, stay there for a while, and then come to the United States. My parents could not decide if they wanted to go to Israel and then the United States. My family are Christians, which was a problem in Russia, but we loved our home.

When my parents were young, people were not nice to them because they were Christians. All their official documents and school papers identified them as Christians. In school sometimes the teacher would spill ink on my mother's homework and tell her, "Your paper is a mess. It has ink all over it. I can't take that. You will have to do it over." Other students put glue in her hair. There was no one to complain to about this bullying, because the teachers would always take the side of the other students. They did not like Christians.

In Russia, all young people must serve in the military. When my father did his service in the army, the officers saw on his papers that he was a Christian. They said, "Oh, you are one of them!" They made his life terrible. They did everything they could to make him stop being a Christian.

At that time, in Russia, people could buy good grades in school, and they could pay someone to get a better job, but not if they were Christian.

When my siblings and I were small, though, it was not so bad for Christians, so my parents could not decide if they wanted to leave Ukraine or not. They decided to let the Bible guide them. My father would open the Bible, and whatever verse he saw first would give them their answer. My father opened the Bible, and the verse told him they should stay and work in Ukraine. They decided to stay in Ukraine.

My family did missionary work. We traveled a lot in our missionary work. We visited orphanages where children didn't have parents and took them gifts. We enjoyed seeing the country, the rural areas. For summer vacation we went camping near Odessa. Our life was very good.

We went to school, and school was good. Our schools in Ukraine were much smaller than schools in America. First grade through eighth grade were in one building. On the first floor were first through fourth grades. On the second floor were fifth through eighth grades. After ninth grade, students could graduate and begin to train for a job or continue in high school to prepare for university. In school I studied Ukrainian, Russian, and French languages. I liked school.

Then my country began to change. It was the time of Glasnost, openness, but now some news was forbidden. People who spoke the truth might disappear; nobody would ever see them again.

Religion became a problem again. People who were not atheist or Russian Orthodox were treated with suspicion. Churches had to be registered. Some churches had to meet in secret in homes because they were not allowed by the government. Our church was registered, but sometimes the police would come to count the people and write down names. My parents began to worry.

In 1997, our uncle in America applied for a visa for us again. The papers from America came in a beautiful envelope. It was very big, with gold letters and beautiful paper. This time the family could go straight to America without staying in Israel. My father decided to open the Bible for guidance again. He opened a new Bible, and the first verse he saw told him it was time to move.

We had to have medical exams and shots and interviews. We had to travel to Kiev for some of our paperwork, and we went by train to Moscow for our medical exams. Anyone who was thirteen or older had to go to the interviews in person and had to sign their own papers, so my older sister and I had to go to the interviews too. It was very exciting, and scary too.

For our interview, we went into a large room with a big long table. There were curtains along the sides of the room. The interviewers sat on one side of the table, and we sat on the other side. We didn't know it, but there were people behind the curtains listening to our interview. When we were finished with our interview, one interviewer said, "I think you are very deserving." Then the people behind the curtains began to clap. They came out from behind the curtains and we met them.

Then we had to get ready to go to America. We were eight people: my parents, my two sisters and me, and our three little brothers. Each of us was allowed two suitcases. Our littlest brother was only three, so he did not have very much to take, but the rest of us had to decide what to take and what to leave. It was hard to decide what to leave behind. Our uncle in America told us what we needed to bring because we would not be able to find it in America and what we should not bring. He told my mother to leave her fur coats behind. "People in America do not like fur coats," he said. So my mother left her coats in Ukraine. She just took one nice fur hat.

My littlest brother tried to bring all of his toy cars in his pockets, but he had to put them back. We sold everything we could not pack or gave it to our relatives. Our parents bought us new shoes and some new clothes for traveling. The last two weeks we stayed with our grandparents, our mother's parents, who were staying in Ukraine. Our other grandparents, our father's parents, went to the USA before us. We had special notebooks for our friends to write us notes so we would never forget them.

Then we had a huge goodbye party. The house was full of people. We had a big dinner with family and friends from church. We were happy and excited, but there was a lot of crying. The church gave us a beautiful new Bible.

Then it was time to leave. One of our uncles was a bus driver and had a big bus, so he drove us to the airport in Kiev. Some people came with us to Kiev to say goodbye at the airport.

The airplane was huge, and noisy. When the plane took off and we looked out the window and saw everything getting smaller and smaller below us, we realized we were really on our way. What was behind us was behind us, and we did not really know what was in front of us. We cried. We couldn't sleep. We flew from Kiev to Amsterdam to New York, and finally to Spokane.

We arrived at 11 p.m. The lights of Spokane looked beautiful in the night. Many, many people came to the airport to meet us. Our uncle's father-in-law came all the way from Canada to greet us. We were introduced to so many people.

Spokane seemed so clean and friendly. The people we met were kind and smiled a lot. We did not understand anything, but everyone seemed very friendly and helpful. The city was overwhelming and confusing because there were signs everywhere in English. We worried a lot about English. None of us had studied English at school.

Our uncle had found us a two-bedroom house, which was much smaller than our home in Ukraine. My sisters and I shared one room. Until we could find a bigger house, everyone had to be good and share. We did our homework in the kitchen and helped each other.

World Relief had everything ready for us: my parents' work permits, our records, everything. We registered for school right away. We worried about what we would do in school without understanding English.

The first day of school we had to take a test. We didn't know any English, so the English test was over very fast. We could not answer any questions.

I did very well on the number parts of the math test, so they put me in a math class with American students. I couldn't understand anything the teacher said! Then the school moved me back to an ESL math class, so I could learn enough English to understand the math book and the math teacher.

At first it was like being a baby again; we had to start over and learn everything. Slowly we started to learn English and understand.

## Epilogue

In high school my sisters and I studied to be nursing assistants at the Spokane Skills Center. When we graduated, we went to college to study nursing. My sisters and I all have jobs in the medical field now. My parents and brothers have good jobs too. Twenty-one years after we arrived in the USA, we are all married, with happy families. We are still active in our church, where I sing in the choir. We have had hard times; my older sister was diagnosed with cancer and told she might die and would never have a child, but she is still alive and has a beautiful child. They are our miracles. God has blessed us.

# Slava

**Ukraine**
**US Entry: 1995**

I grew up in Kherson, Ukraine. I had a good life with good friends. We hiked and camped, spending a lot of our time by the river, in the forest, outside in nature. I was happy in my life, but my parents decided we would have a better life in America. We were Christians, and because we were Christian, we were enemies of the state. Christians had to register with the government. We could be arrested or even killed because of our religion. Ukraine was not a good place to be a Christian at that time.

I was fifteen, almost sixteen, when my parents dropped the bomb on me that we would go to America. They had done the paperwork and interviews and they had already made the decision before they said anything to me. That is the way it is in my culture. Parents make the decisions and tell you what to do, and you do it. My sister was so little that it did not matter to her, but I was not happy. I had my friends. I had my girlfriend. I was ready to do my military service and start my adult life. Kherson was where I lived my whole life, and I felt like I was leaving my whole life behind. There was nothing I could do because I was not eighteen; I had to do what my parents told me to do.

I had one summer, just three months, to say goodbye to my country and get ready to go to America. When I told my friends, they told me to stay and said they would help me live on my own. We spent that summer camping and partying, but it was sad. I was leaving my whole childhood behind. I grew up in that town. My father and I had built our house with our own hands. I was leaving all my memories, good and bad. I had to obey my parents, but I planned to come back in two years, when I was eighteen.

The day before we left, I told my friends, "Do not come to say goodbye. It will be hard enough."

We flew from Kherson to Moscow. In Moscow we had our final interviews, physical checkup, and shots—lots of shots. Then we flew from Moscow to Germany, then to New York.

We arrived in New York at night. The city lights were amazing. We spent the night in New York. Everything I knew about America was from movies, Hollywood stuff. I thought everything in America would be fancy and beautiful like the lights of New York City. The next day we flew to Spokane, and it was a rude awakening.

My cousins met us at the airport, and we stayed with them for a couple of weeks. Then we found an apartment for ourselves. My town in Ukraine was not considered a big town, but it was bigger than Spokane. We had big, beautiful, solid, brick houses. The only wooden buildings were garages, barns, or sheds. We had tall buildings, nine or more stories tall. In Spokane the houses were made of wood, and so small, like miniature houses. I asked myself, "Where am I?" I asked my parents, "How is this a better life? How can we trade that for this?" I could not understand how this life was better.

I started walking around the city, exploring the area. The grocery stores were the best, most amazing shock. The food was so good! There was every kind of food. I ate so many bananas. We could not get bananas in Ukraine.

The American people were so confusing. Everywhere I went, people were always smiling, for no reason. I thought,

*Are you drunk?* Everyone else seemed so happy all the time. But I missed my friends, and language was a huge barrier.

In Ukraine, I studied English, but it was different from the English in America. This was a shock. All of my life was a roller coaster. I started school a couple of weeks after we arrived, but I did not want to study English. I did not want to study at all. Our school system in Ukraine is different. After ninth grade, we can go to high school to prepare for college or trade school to prepare for a job. I did not want to be back in high school. American school was very confusing, but the school lunches were awesome.

I wanted to work and earn money so I could go back to Ukraine. I started doing a morning paper route. I woke up at 3 a.m. and delivered papers. After a while I had three paper routes. I delivered papers seven days a week. After school I worked in a factory from 4 p.m. to midnight. I gave part of my money to my family, to help pay for our home and food, because that is the way we do it in my culture, and I saved the rest of my money to go back to Ukraine.

After a year, my girlfriend in Ukraine broke up with me. It is hard to have a relationship so far apart. I changed my mind about going back to Ukraine. I decided I would stay in America and make my life here.

I made friends, other students from other countries who were learning English. I got along with the American students as long as they did not try to pick on us. Sometimes they gave us looks, and sometimes they said bad words that I did not really understand, but if they left me alone, I left them alone. My English improved, and I was able to take classes at the skills center. I started to study in the automotive repair program. That gave me the idea to go to college and someday have my own shop.

# Epilogue

After high school I went to college and became certified in automotive mechanics, auto body repair, and automotive electrical systems. I also got married, which was the best decision I ever made. After college I moved to Seattle, but I did not work in an automotive shop. I worked doing maintenance for an apartment building. Every week I had to write up a report—it was just like being in school again! After a couple of years, I moved back to Spokane and worked in construction. Then I got a job working at the Spalding Auto Parts and Salvage. I do not like to do the same thing every day, I like a challenge and I like to do something different. In 2012, I started working as an over-the-road truck driver. This is a good job for me. Every day is different: new roads, new loads, meeting new people, and plenty of challenges.

I have bought some property where I am building a home and a shop, where I can do semitruck repair. I will finally have my own shop.

I have two sons now, and I tell them, *Do not lose this opportunity. Work smart, not hard.* My dream for my sons is that they get the best education they can have, to do something with their lives that makes them happy. One son likes to draw and wants to do animation. The other likes big, heavy machinery. Whatever they want to do, I want them to follow their dreams.

I would like Americans to know that we immigrants are not bad. People say we are taking their jobs, but how are we taking their jobs? They can apply for the same jobs we apply for. We are doing the jobs they do not want to do. Just because we came from another country does not make us bad. We came here for better lives, and we work for that better life. The US economy runs on immigrant labor. Some American people do not want to work, but we do. I have had to work side jobs, hard jobs, to feed my family. I work, I do my job, I pay my taxes. As a truck driver I am on the road seven days and home three. When I am home, I am with my family. We have a happy life. That is the American Dream.

•

CHAPTER 14

# MOLDOVA

....................................................

## A Few Facts about Moldova

**AREA:** 13,067 square miles (33,843 sq. km)

**POPULATION:** 3.02 million

**LANGUAGES:** Moldovan, Romanian, Russian, Ukranian, and Gagauz (Turkic dialect)

**RELIGIONS:** Christianity, Judaism, Islam, and other religions

## A Little History

In the early Common Era, Moldova was controlled by the Romans, then the Byzantines, and other invaders. Moldova was part of the Ottoman Empire from the early 1500s until 1812, when the Ottomans surrendered Moldova to the Russians.

Most of the people of Moldova are ethnic Moldovans, who are closely related to Romanians. The Romanian and Moldovan languages are extremely similar.

Moldova declared independence from the USSR in 1991. Soon afterward, ethnic Russians in the Transnistria area on the border of Moldova and Ukraine declared their own independence. In 1994 Moldova granted Transnistria autonomy, meaning the people could rule themselves, but there are still tensions in that area and the Russian military keeps troops there. Moldova remains one of the poorest countries in Europe.

## Why Do People Leave?

During the Soviet era, people had very little religious freedom. Protestant Christian and Jewish Moldovans in particular have left as religious refugees. Life was also difficult because of tensions between Russia and Moldova that weakened the economy. According to the United Nations Population Fund, the population of Moldova has decreased rapidly between 1989 and 2019.

# Andrei

**Moldova**
**US Entry: 1998**

For the first fifteen years of my life, I was raised in Sinjerei, in the center of the Republic of Moldova. I am the middle child, and only boy, of a large family of five kids. My mother is a very big believer in God, a churchgoing woman, so we were raised with very positive values and many traditions that had been kept and passed down from generation to generation.

I was born in the USSR, but in 1991 the USSR broke apart and Moldova became an independent country. We were supposed to have more freedom when Moldova became independent, but we really did not have more freedom. In the USSR days, I wore a uniform to school every day, and students wore the red bandana of the Young Pioneers [a Soviet youth organization] every day. After independence we could wear what we wanted, but in other ways Moldovan people did not have freedom. Russia controlled trade with Moldova. The Russians would not buy Moldovan wine anymore, so many farmers had to stop growing grapes and start growing corn. Most of the people in Moldova were Orthodox Christians or nonbelievers, and they did not approve of other religions like Baptists [a Protestant branch of Christianity]. My family were Baptists.

When I was very young, maybe five or six years old, my mother's relatives started leaving Moldova and going to the USA for religious freedom. My mother comes from a big family with ten children. We were farmers, and farmers need big

The Young Pioneers was an organization for Soviet youth ages nine to fourteen that aimed to strengthen loyalty to communism and the Soviet Union.

families to help with the farm. Some of my uncles went from the USSR to Cuba, and then took a boat from Cuba to Canada, and then traveled to America in 1988.

We had big parties to say goodbye to family members as they left to go to America. I was raised with the idea that someday I would go to America too. As I was growing up, everything inside me was calling for me to learn and experience more in life. My mother started the paperwork to go to America, but it took many years for the process to be completed. We talked about moving to America as a family. We always knew that our father was the one who did not want to go to America. He was a not a Christian believer. He was a patriot to who loved his country. Leaving Moldova was very hard for him, but he loved his wife and his children.

Finally, after ten years of waiting, it was our turn to go to America. This was the biggest opportunity, the biggest excitement for me, because this meant I could explore and learn more.

When we received our visas, we sold everything. We had a big goodbye party with our family and friends. We drove to Ukraine. From Ukraine we flew to New York and then Salt Lake City, and finally, our landing place in the United States was the city of Spokane, Washington. This was where a large wave of Eastern European religious refugees had chosen to call home. We arrived on July 15, 1998.

Our relatives who lived in Spokane and their friends were waiting for us at the airport. We were so happy to see them, and they were so happy to see us. We had a big welcome to America.

Our relatives lived in an apartment complex. They had put our names down for an apartment as soon as they knew we were coming, so we had an apartment near them. Spokane seemed like a big city. Sinjerei was not so big. At first, I would just sit and watch people. I wanted to absorb everything, like a little kid. There was so much to learn and so much to see.

The apartment complex had a basketball court, and I learned to play basketball that summer. The American kids in the neighborhood were friendly and helped me learn English. I made friends. In the fall school started, so my younger sister and I went to high school. In Moldova I studied Russian, Moldovan, and French. Now I started to study English. Within six months of moving to the United States, I felt like I had learned enough English to be comfortable speaking the language. I began to feel comfortable in the USA and had some good friends. The best thing ever was coming to America.

## Epilogue

Right after my high school graduation, I decided to join the United States Navy. My father did not want me to join the military, because his experience in the Soviet military was not good.

He helped me to train physically for boot camp so it would not be so hard on me physically.

At that point I realized I had not fully grasped the English language. To make matters even more challenging, the war of 9/11 [the 2001 US invasion of Afghanistan] had just started, and I was sent straight to Saudi Arabia right after boot camp. Most of my shipmates did not accept a former Soviet, a foreigner, serving alongside them, which taught me a very hard lesson mentally. I did not see a break until the time I separated from the Navy. I found peace in conducting the ship's helm during my time of service and really connecting with the water and its energy. Upon returning from the Gulf War, the ship returned to its home base of San Diego, this is when I fell in love with San Diego and have called it my home ever since. To this day, I could not have asked for a better place to reside, work, and grow each day than the beautiful and sunny San Diego.

After separating from the service, I quickly took advantage of the benefits gathered in the service and completed my degree in environmental services/HVAC&R, [heating, ventilation and air conditioning, and refrigeration] and worked as a mechanical design drafter. After six years, I made the decision to go back to school. I completed my bachelor's degree in business management, which used the rest of my education benefits from the service.

While I was studying and working, I started another career as well. People had often told me I looked good in photographs, so I decided to try working as a model. At first, I worked with modeling agencies, and that was no good. Then I started to work with photographers and built my portfolio. I worked successfully in high fashion modeling for a few years. Being involved in the entertainment industry of high fashion modeling, I have had the opportunity to interact with some of the greatest artists, and this has taught me some of my most valuable lessons that carry on throughout my life and career. I know now that if not for my modeling career, I would not have reached my destined path or experienced the difficulties I had to encounter, which made me stronger.

I have learned that happiness starts from within ourselves, not from the outside. So many of us have this concept completely backwards, thinking the more we have, the happier we will be. But materialistic things are very short lived, and although things may bring excitement momentarily, ultimately the excitement ends, there is nothing more to fill the void within, and therein lies the problem. The joy of your heart grows from projecting joy to everybody around you. I am enjoying my journey each step of the way and look forward to what each day may bring.

EUROPE

ASIA

Kazakhstan

Kyrgyzstan

AFRICA

*CHAPTER 15*

# KAZAKHSTAN
# AND
# KYRGYZSTAN

·······························································

## A Few Facts about Kazakhstan

**AREA:** 1.05 million square miles (2.72 million sq. km)

**POPULATION:** 18.76 million

**LANGUAGES:** Kazakh and Russian

**RELIGIONS:** Islam, Christianity, and Judaism

# A Few Facts about Kyrgyzstan

**AREA:** 77,199 square miles (199,945 sq. km)

**POPULATION:** 6.59 million

**LANGUAGES:** Kyrgyz, Uzbek, and Russian

**RELIGIONS:** Islam, with some Christianity, Judaism, Buddhism, and other religions

# A Little History

The early people of Kyrgyzstan and Kazakhstan were nomadic tribes from Europe and Asia. In the 700s and 800s CE, Arabs conquered much of central Asia, including what is now Kazakhstan and Kyrgyzstan, and many Kazakh and Kyrgyz people converted to Islam. Later, Genghis Khan conquered this area, and the Kazakh and Kyrgyz people were under Mongol rule until the Russian Empire claimed this region in the late 1800s. Russian farmers moved into Kazakhstan and Kyrgyzstan looking for pasture and farmland, pushing the nomadic people off their land and into the mountains. In both Kyrgyzstan and Kazakhstan, Russian and Ukrainian migration led to cultural friction, but resistance to Russian rule was unsuccessful. Thousands of Kyrgyz and Kazakh people fled to China, but many did not survive the journey.

During the Russian revolution and civil war (1917–1922), the Kyrgyz and Kazakh people did not support the Communists, but the Red Army occupied Kazakhstan. Kyrgyzstan and Kazakhstan both became Soviet republics in 1936. The Soviet government tried to force the nomadic Kyrgyz and Kazakh people to settle into farming or urban life. Under communism the land was owned and controlled by the government. Under this system, the Kyrgyz and Kazakh people lost their lifestyle. In both countries the non-Russian population dropped quickly. A 1953 Soviet agricultural program opened up northern Kazakhstan's grasslands to wheat farming by ethnic Russians, leading to ecological destruction of the grasslands and additional friction between Russians and Kazakhs.

When the USSR began to break apart, Kyrgyzstan and Kazakhstan declared independence. Kyrgyzstan became independent August 31, 1991, and Kazakhstan became independent December 16, 1991.

## Why Do People Leave?

When Kyrgyzstan and Kazakhstan became independent countries, the balance of power between ethnic Russians and ethnic Kyrgyz and Kazakhs changed. Kyrgyz and Kazakh people wanted to use their own languages instead of Russian, regain their cultural identities, and freely practice religion. In both countries Islam is the majority religion. Ethnic Russians who were also Christians began to feel unwelcome and unsafe. Some rejoined family in other parts of the former USSR. Others left for other countries as religious refugees.

# Fedor

**Kazakhstan**
**US Entry: 1998**

I was born in Kazakhstan when Kazakhstan was part of the USSR. My father's family were Germans, but they were sent to Siberia by Stalin. My father was born in Siberia.

All young people must serve in the military in Russia. When my father did his military service, he was sent to Kazakhstan. He got sick in Kazakhstan and went to the hospital, and that is where he met my mother. My mother worked in the hospital. They got married and stayed in Kazakhstan.

I have a big family: two sisters, six brothers, and me. I lived in a rural area in Kazakhstan. We lived in the mountains. We had horses, cattle, and dogs. We had a big garden. My family raised most of our own food. We carried water from the well, and we did everything by hand. We did not have machines like a washing machine or a dishwasher. We worked hard, but our life had a lot of freedom.

In the summer we took the cattle into the mountains to graze. The cattle knew the routine. They knew where to go to find grass. We rode our horses and followed the cattle all summer. In the summer we lived in a yurt, in nature. We wore leather clothes because leather is strong, cool in the summer, and warm in the winter. In the fall, we came back to home to go to school.

Our school was small. Elementary students went to school in the mornings, and high school students went to school in the afternoon.

We woke up in the morning and milked the cows. We would drink the still-warm milk for breakfast with fresh bread and butter. We made butter by putting the cream in a big jar and shaking it until the cream made butter.

My parents did not push us to go to school. They were not fans of school. My family is Christian. The government put a lot of pressure on people to not be Christians. The USSR did not like Christians. Kazakhstan became independent from the USSR in 1991. The Kazakh people are mostly Muslim, so the Kazakh government wanted people to be Muslim, not Christian.

My family decided to leave Kazakhstan as religious refugees.

We applied for visas to Germany and to the United States. My father's family moved to Germany. My mother's family moved to the United States.

One day when I was fourteen years old, we got two big, beautiful, fancy envelopes. We were accepted by Germany and the United States on the same day. Mother made a big meal with a fancy bread. This was exciting news. My parents had to decide where to go. My parents heard that the USA was more open to immigrants. Germany was not so open. It was hard to become a citizen in Germany. My mother wanted to go to the United States where her brother and parents were. My father agreed.

First, we had to go to Moscow for interviews and medical exams. We each had a big IOM bag. We went to a big building like a bank. We waited and then they called us into a big room and asked us questions. After that we had our medical exams. We were in Moscow for a week. We went to the Moscow Zoo; it was amazing. Then they told us we could go to America. We went home and prepared to leave.

The International Organization for Migration is an organization that works with refugees. Each refugee receives a large plastic bag where they are encouraged to store their important documents such as refugee identification cards, their TSA (Transportation Security Administration) letter, photo identification, passports, and birth certificates.

We had to sell everything to buy tickets to go to the USA. We sold the house and moved in with my uncle. We sold all the horses and cattle. The saddest was selling our cow that had twin calves. Our neighbor wanted the cow but not the two calves. They said they would take them to the market and sell them for shish kabob. Everything we did not sell, we gave away. We only took some clothes. Our family in America told us that anything we needed, we could get in America. We each had a suitcase.

I was excited to go but sad to say goodbye to everything I knew and the place I was born. We did not know much about the United States. Everything we knew was from other people. We did not have a TV. My mother said we would never have to carry water again. We would never have to wash our clothes by hand again, because in America there are machines that do that for you.

Our uncle rented a big hall, and we had a big party to say goodbye to our friends and family. Some people did not believe we were going to America.

Our uncle drove us to Almaty, the old capital city of Kazakhstan. Then we took a train to Moscow. Our parents told us not to tell anyone that we were going to America, because they would want to steal from us. It was unusual to see such a big family traveling together. We met other children on the train and told them, "We are going to America." The children told their parents, but nobody robbed us.

We took the underground metro from the train station to the airport. I saw a Black person for the first time. My parents said, "Don't stare." But it was the first time I ever saw someone whose skin was so dark. I had heard there were people who had different-colored skin, but this was the first time I saw it.

We took a big Aeroflot plane from Moscow to New York. I watched Mr. Bean on the television on the plane. It was so funny. Mr. Bean doesn't talk, so I didn't have to understand English. I was very tired when we arrived in New York. We changed to another plane, and that night we arrived in Spokane. My mother's brother and parents and many friends from church were there to meet us. We were excited to see so many people waiting for us.

On the drive from the airport to Spokane, our uncle told us about the difference between kilometers and miles. We stayed at our uncle's house until we could find a house to rent. The first night, everyone just slept. We were very tired. The next morning, we all waited in line to take our first hot showers in America.

Everything was so different. Our uncle's house was so big. They had a TV and a washing machine. World Relief found a house for us to rent, a duplex across the street from a park. They brought us mattresses so we each had a bed. They helped us get furniture and what we needed in the house. We started to learn about our new home, Spokane.

Someone told us, "If people put something out by the side of the road, you can just take it for free." My brother and I saw bicycles by the side of the road and took them. I felt so lucky—until a few minutes later the police came and took the bikes back to their owner. I had a lot to learn about life in America.

Soon it was time to go to school. I was worried. I didn't know anyone. I didn't have friends yet. I didn't know English. I thought people would think I was stupid.

The hardest part of school was the schedule. There were a lot of rules, and I had to be in the right class at the right time. I had homework too. My family did not really understand how important school was. School was hard.

The best part of school was school lunch. The food was very different, but I liked it. Pizza was strange at first. What was this bread with lots of stuff on top? Tater tots were so good.

I had a photography class. It was great. I learned how to use a camera and I could go all over the school taking pictures. I had woodworking class and learned how to use machines to make things from wood.

After a while I made some friends and learned how to live in America.

## Epilogue

Now I am married and have a son of my own. My life is good.

In Kazakhstan, we did not have a good quality of life. We did not have opportunity. In Kazakhstan if you do not know someone who can get you a better job, you are stuck where you are, and your children are stuck. When I came to the USA, I did not understand how important education is. Good grades mean a good education, and with hard work a good education means a good life.

Some people merged into their new life in America easily, and some did not understand the opportunity they had to get a better life. In the beginning I did not understand. There was a lot of peer pressure to not behave, and I was not a good student. Whatever people are surrounded by, what they live with, they think is just normal, until someone helps them see a better way.

When we meet different people, we can see a different quality of life. When we help the people around us, we create a better society. I want my son to move up in the world, to live in a better world, and to have a better life than mine. If my son does not have a better life than me, I will feel like I failed.

Right now, I am studying to be a police officer because I want to give back to my community. I am studying, reading, doing physical training.

# Andrey

**Kyrgyzstan**
**US Entry: 1996**

I was born in Bishkek, the capital city of Kyrgyzstan, in the Soviet Union. A long time ago, my family came from Russia, but that was many generations ago. Bishkek is a big city with many tall apartment buildings, and we lived in one of those tall apartment towers. Many families with children lived in the apartment towers.

On a normal day in Bishkek, I woke up early and went to school. At the end of the school day, I came home and helped my mother with whatever she needed. Then I went out to play with my friends. A lot of children lived in those apartments. It was normal for us to stay outside until dark. My friends and I played outside building forts and little huts. We went to the river and got dirty in the mud. We ran and played games. We had too much fun and got in trouble sometimes. We used our imaginations, figured out how things worked, and learned from experience.

My mother comes from a very big family, and most of her family moved to the United States. My mother always told my brother and me, "Learn English!" She said, "We will move to the United States."

When Kyrgyzstan became independent, life started to become harder for Russian-speaking people. The government made a law that said everyone must speak the Kyrgyz language or leave. We were required to study Kyrgyz in school, but I argued, "No. I need to learn English." My teachers asked me why, and I said, "I am moving to America someday."

Schools in Kyrgyzstan are different from schools in America. We had to sit up straight, with our arms folded in front of us on our desk. If we did not behave, the teachers would smack our hands. If we did not write perfectly, they would smack our hands and make us do the work over.

One day when I was ten years old, my mother said, "We are moving to America now."

We sold everything we had and packed our bags. We took a train to Moscow. My two younger brothers, who were nine and four years old; my mother; my stepfather; and I rode the train for four days. We got on a plane and flew to New York. Getting on the plane was the scariest and coolest time of my life. On the plane we watched the movie *Titanic* all the way across the ocean. In New York someone helped us finds our next plane, and then we flew to Spokane.

My uncles and their families met us at the airport in Spokane. We arrived at night and went to the apartment my uncles had found for us. Everything was so different—the cars were different, the houses were different. Everything was so clean. There was so much freedom, and people could go where they want and do what they want. Everyone was always smiling. People always asked, "How are you?" I wondered, *Why are you asking how I am? Why do you care how I am?* I did not understand that this was just how Americans start conversations.

We had studied English in Kyrgyzstan, but we didn't really know English, just a few words. I learned more English from watching TV. I had to put it all together. Understanding English was hard.

I was just a kid, so my biggest concerns were food and sweets. I remember eating bananas for the first time. People take things for granted, but in Kyrgyzstan we never had bananas. The only people who had bananas in Kyrgyzstan were like friends with the president or something.

Going to school was exciting and scary. I went to middle school, and my teacher was so kind to me. In the USA, schools are so nice. Teachers talk to students and try to understand the students. My English teachers helped me a lot.

In school I met a lot of other Russian-speaking students. I did not expect to meet other Russian students in American schools. Many Russian refugees came to Spokane about the same time my family came to the United States.

When I went to high school, I felt like everyone was looking at me like I was different. The school was so big! I got lost a lot. Some people did not like "Russians." Sometimes I felt angry because I felt like people turned their backs if the Russian students were being bullied, but if the Russians fought back, we got in trouble. I was angry because I felt like I didn't do anything to them, so I did not understand why they bullied us.

Most of the Russian-speaking students had to work to help our families pay the bills. Our parents had jobs and we had jobs; everyone worked. Many of us had jobs delivering newspapers. We got up at 3 a.m. to deliver the papers. After delivering the papers we would sleep a little, then go to school. I was so tired that I fell asleep in first period a lot, but family comes first. Some teachers did not understand why we were so tired all the time.

My PE teacher told me I should join the wrestling team, so I joined. The first year I did not do well at wrestling matches; I only won one match. I was tired of getting beaten, so I wanted to quit, but my coach said, "Keep trying. You can do this. You will become good." I kept going and I made friends, and the second year I made varsity. I wrestled varsity for three years.

In Kyrgyzstan I liked photography. In Spokane I took a photography class, and at first the teacher did not like me, but I like photography. I made friends in photography class too.

After a while my photography teacher started to like me, and he was like a grandfather to me. He was very funny; we joked together all the time. If I said, "Oh God," he would say, "Yes?" He helped me with everything and even helped me find a job working for a photographer. I joined the yearbook class, too. I became the chief photographer for the yearbook. Soon I knew everyone, and everyone knew me.

Getting involved in school helped me feel like a part of the school community. Being a part of a team took the anger away from me and got rid of the negativity. When people had a chance to get to know me, their attitudes changed. Now I understand that there are good people and bad people in every group. We all have the same choices to make. Will we do good or will we do bad?

## Epilogue

After graduation, I went to California to go to college to be an auto mechanic. Every time we move, or change jobs, or start a business, we have to start over again. I believe that every person gets the same opportunities to choose good or bad. We have to be ready to work for what we want. People should make good choices and be good to each other. I see now that my wrestling coach and my photography teacher helped me in so many ways, more than just school. They respected me, and they helped me so much. I try to always respect everybody. That person you disrespect today may be the person who saves your life tomorrow. I tell my children to work for what they want, respect everyone, and give without expecting anything in return.

Now I have my own trucking business with twenty-seven trucks. I also have a private bodyguard/personal security business. I can't complain! I have a good life. I have two children I love more than life. My family means everything to me.

EUROPE

Bosnia and
Herzegovina

Kosovo

ATLANTIC
OCEAN

AFRICA

CHAPTER 16

# BOSNIA AND HERZEGOVINA AND KOSOVO

## A Few Facts about Bosnia and Herzegovina

**AREA:** 19,772 square miles (51,209 sq. km)

**POPULATION:** 3.41 million

**LANGUAGES:** Bosnian, Croatian, and Serbian

**RELIGIONS:** Islam, Christianity, and other religions

# A Few Facts about Kosovo

**AREA:** 4,210 square miles (10,905 sq. km)

**POPULATION:** 1.81 million

**LANGUAGES:** Albanian and Serbian

**RELIGIONS:** Islam and Christianity

## A Little History

Bosnia and Herzegovina and Kosovo have all been under the control of different nations at different times, and this has caused them to develop diverse cultures. Early in the Common Era, most Europeans converted to Christianity. When the Ottoman Empire controlled the region in the fifteenth century, many Bosnians and Kosovars converted to Islam.

In 1908 Bosnia and Herzegovina and Kosovo were annexed by the Austro-Hungarian government. World War I started in 1914 when Archduke Franz Ferdinand of Austria was assassinated by a Serbian nationalist in Sarajevo, the capital of Bosnia. The Serbian nationalists were fighting to free Bosnia and Herzegovina from the control of the Austro-Hungarian government.

At the end of World War I, Bosnia and Herzegovina and Kosovo were included in the new Kingdom of Serbs, Croats, and Slovenes. This new country was governed by Serbian king Alexander I. Hoping to end conflict between the different ethnic groups—including Serbs, Croats, Slovenes, and Bosnians—he renamed the country Yugoslavia in 1929. He wanted these groups to unite as Yugoslavians. During World War II, conflict between the groups fueled killing. The casualties from the war are estimated anywhere from half a million to over one million. In 1945, after World War II, this kingdom became the Socialist Federal Republic of Yugoslavia. Under the Socialist government of Yugoslavia, Yugoslavia's diverse religions and ethnicities coexisted.

In the late 1980s, Communist governments in Eastern Europe began to collapse, and the republics of the USSR began to break apart. In 1991 different regions of the Republic of Yugoslavia declared independence. In Kosovo, ethnic Albanians tried to form their own independent republic, but Yugoslavia's Serbian government refused to recognize the region's independence. The majority of Bosnia and Herzegovina voted for independence in 1992.

Serbs, most of whom were Orthodox Christian, wanted Serbian control of Bosnia and Herzegovina and Kosovo. Croats, who were mostly Catholic, wanted Croatian control. Soon the region dissolved into war and ethnic cleansing.

In Bosnia, Serb forces killed one hundred thousand people, mostly Bosnian Muslims. More than two million people became refugees. In Kosovo, six hundred thousand Kosovars were forced to leave their country and another eleven thousand people, mostly Muslims, were killed by Serbs during the 1990s.

The UN charged Serb leaders Radovan Karadzic, Ratko Mladic, and Slobodan Milosevic with genocide and crimes against humanity. Milosevic died in prison in 2006 before the end of his trial; Karadzic and Mladic were found guilty and sentenced to life in prison.

## Why Did People Leave?

People left Bosnia and Kosovo to escape the violence and ethnic cleansing. Many found temporary refuge in Germany and other European countries. When the war ended, they had nothing to go home to and resettled as refugees in other countries.

# Fedja

**Bosnia and Herzegovina**
**US entry: 1995**

I was born in the city Banja Luka in the former Yugoslavia. Banja Luka is a fairly large city, full of culture and history. I grew up with my mom and grandmother. My parents divorced when I was two years old. We lived in a large apartment complex in a part of the city called Nova Varoš (New Borough). My school was only a short three-minute walk from my home, and all my friends lived in the neighborhood. Most of them lived in my building. We would play in the green areas between the buildings or at the basketball court.

My neighborhood was very close to the city's downtown. I would often go with my grandma to the farmer's market and shopping centers, run errands, and then go for walks through the park. We would go to a restaurant and get ćevapi (Bosnian burgers) or stop at the sweetshop for ice cream or cake. My grandma would take me to art galleries, museums, or children's theater. We were very close. My mom would take me out to the evening concerts that my grandma wasn't interested in. This woke up my love for music. I started piano lessons, and later I switched to guitar.

Every summer and every winter when school was not in session, my grandma and I would travel to our cabin in the mountains, and I would get to see my friends who lived in different parts of the country. It was a large vacation community full of children my age, and we spent summer and winter vacations together. We would go hiking in the mountains and ride horses. In the evenings we would play soccer until it got too dark, and then we would build bonfires, watch stars, and sing songs or listen to the cassette tapes of our favorite bands. Our cabin was also very close to the small town where my grandma was born and where most of my cousins lived. I saw them and spent time with them every summer and every winter. My mom would also take me to the Adriatic coast on a summer vacation nearly every year. I learned to swim in the Adriatic Sea.

We first learned about the war by watching it on TV. In 1991 there was trouble in Croatia, and suddenly there were Croatian refugees in our hometown. The big sports arena where I used to go to concerts became a refugee camp. There were tall fences around the place, and sometimes when I walked by, I would see kids playing on the steps.

Once the war started in Bosnia, traveling wasn't safe anymore. Our city became a military hub with tanks and army trucks coming and going nearly every day. The fighting never happened in my city, but we were constantly exposed to the aftermath. When I was with my grandma, she wouldn't stop watching the news, which kept up with latest battles, death tolls, and massacres of civilians. My mom tried to protect me from all of it; I was only thirteen. She never wanted me to develop hate for other religions. My mother and I never watched the news together.

The city lost power, so we lived by candlelight the first year of the war. There was no heat. Many elderly people froze to death in their apartments. There was also very little food in the stores, and it was very expensive. Later there was no food at all. The apartments that were not ground level lost running water, so cooking and showering and washing clothes were difficult. We had a small fluorescent lamp hooked up to a car battery for lights and later another one for a radio. By this time most of my friends had left the country, and the city was full of refugees. I felt uncomfortable in my own home, but I didn't want to go outside. I retreated into my own world of music and books. I locked myself in my apartment and would only go out when I needed to go to school. When I came home, I cleaned the entire apartment because it gave me something to do and spent the rest of the day reading, doing homework, and practicing guitar.

I thought, "This cannot last." I kept thinking that one day I would wake up and the war would be over, and all my friends would come back.

My mom decided it was time to leave when I was about to get registered for military service. I was sixteen. My mom didn't want me to go to war. I remember my mom and grandma arguing because my mom wanted us to leave and Grandma was against it. I felt like I was caught in the middle. I didn't want to leave, but my mom explained to me that we had no choice. The registration day for the mandatory draft was only a few short months away, and after four years of fighting, the end of the war was nowhere in sight.

By this time, there were already many casualties, and hospitals were filled with men not that much older than me, with missing body parts or severe PTSD. Suicide rates were very high too, and life was nothing like the life we knew before the war. At night we would hear explosions and gunshots. Each day when I came to school, another one of my friends would be missing from class. People were disappearing into the night. One day, a whole group of refugee students from nearby villages came into the classroom. They were new students.

I come from a religiously mixed family. My mom was born into a Greek Orthodox family, and my dad was born into a Muslim family. These things didn't matter in Bosnia before the war because in 1970s and 1980s Yugoslavia was a united country with people of multiple religions and nationalities. Once nationalism took over in the early 1990s and war broke out, religion mattered. Ultimately the war became a religious war: Christians versus Muslims. My mom felt like we didn't belong to either side. Although I didn't have many connections to my dad's side of the family, I carried his last name, which was Muslim, and even though we didn't practice any religion, in the eyes of everyone else, that didn't matter. My last name was Muslim, so I was Muslim.

Before we left, I spent a lot of time running around with my mom from one administrative office to the other, changing my last name to my mother's last name and then changing all my documents to my new name.

My last summer at the cabin, the vacation community had become a military outpost, so I made friends with soldiers. When I returned to the city, my mom had already sold some things, and we were packing. My grandmother helped us contact her family members who lived in Serbia, where we planned to go while we waited for visas to the Netherlands. That was the original plan.

We were only able to bring clothes, some family photos, and documents—and I brought a few cassettes with my favorite music. My mom kept telling me to leave things. "We are only taking our clothes and toiletries." It was like going on vacation, only this time I was bringing a lot more clothes. I couldn't bring my guitar, piano, or record collection. My bike had already been stolen. I was leaving my few remaining friends and all of my family. My grandmother was staying behind to keep the apartment from being taken away by the refugees and to keep our cabin from being seized by the military. I felt like I would never get to see any of it again. I was right.

I felt lost. I felt afraid. My mom kept telling me about the family that I was about to meet and how they were related to my grandmother. I kept thinking that they wouldn't like me, that they would hate my long hair and my Metallica T-shirt and my pierced ears. I was mad. I cried. I told her I didn't want to go, that she should just go by herself.

Then it was time to leave. My best friend, Suzana, who lived next door and who I was secretly in love with, helped my mom and me carry our oversized bags of clothes to the bus station. I remember her crying and me crying. I remember our kiss, and her walking away as the bus pulled out of station.

I remember just a few hours later, traveling through the war-torn countryside with nothing but military outposts and barbed wire on both sides of the highway.

Crossing the border from Bosnia into Serbia was very nerve wracking even though we had all our papers in order. The bus was traveling through parts of the country that were completely destroyed by war, past ghost towns and ruins of homes destroyed by bombs and fires.

We left Bosnia in the fall of 1994 and stayed with family in Vojvodina, Serbia. Once we arrived and settled in Serbia, I felt like maybe this was where we should stay. Sometimes I felt like we were just visiting family, and maybe my mom would change her mind and we would return home.

As time passed, though, I felt more and more anxious. Our visas were nowhere in sight, and we were quickly wearing out our welcome with our distant relatives. Serbia was not directly in war at that time but was facing economic hardship due to embargoes, and our hosts were barely scraping by, so feeding extra two people was not easy. I felt like I was a burden.

That winter, we planned to cross the border into Hungary where my grandfather (my mom's dad) was waiting for us to help get us into Croatia. When we attempted to enter Hungary by bus, thinking that we had the correct documents, we were taken off the bus and escorted back to the Serbian border by Hungarian border patrol. We took a cab back to a small town where the cab driver told us that he could smuggle us across the border, because he had a friend who worked at the border, but we had to wait for his shift. That actually worked, and when we crossed the border, he drove us to Budapest where we met with my grandfather.

In Budapest, we got on a bus that took us to Zagreb, Croatia. The border patrol had guns, and they would stand at the door while another person with a gun would check everyone's papers. The European Union had closed borders for Bosnian refugees, and we were denied entrance into all the countries where we applied for visas. After waiting seven months in Croatia, we completed the immigration process for the US and got our immigration status approved by the US government. We were granted refugee visas in June of 1995.

Then we were on our way to the USA. Our only layover was in Milan, Italy. From Milan we flew to New York, where we caught a connecting flight to Des Moines, Iowa and from there to Salt Lake City, and then to Spokane. We came to Spokane because this is where our sponsor lived and where the World Relief agency was.

At first, we lived with our sponsor, who lived far away in Spokane Valley, and nothing was within walking distance. I spent so much time in the backseat of a car. Back home we didn't even own a car. We didn't need one. In Banja Luka everything was within walking distance. The only time we got on a bus or a train was if we went on vacation somewhere. Later we had our own apartment.

I remember going to many offices and meeting people from World Relief who wanted us to go straight to work. I remember many fights between my mom and the people at the agency and her crying, "We need to learn English first!" They wanted me to go to work, but I was only seventeen and I needed to finish school. I worried that she would give up and that we would end up working in some warehouse or factory somewhere without ever learning how to speak English.

Finally, my mother was enrolled in English as a Second Language classes and I was enrolled in high school as a junior. I began the year in ESL English 1 and ended the year in English 4. The next year, my senior year, all my classes were with American kids, people who spoke English as their first language. I began to make some friends and started a band. My mother and I got jobs. We began to make lives for ourselves in Spokane.

## Epilogue

Life was difficult for a long time, but my life is good now, and I try to give back and to help people whenever I can. My mother and grandmother live in Portland, near enough that I can see them often. I am married now. My wife has her degree in early childhood education. I do in-home care for people with developmental disabilities as I near completion of my BA in musicology and ethnomusicology. My dream is to get a MA in music education and to start my own music program for children who are immigrants, who are high risk, or who have learning disabilities—in other words, those who often don't have the access or privilege to enroll in regular music programs.

# Sanel

**Bosnia and Herzegovina**
**US Entry: 1999**

I am from Bosanski Petrovac in Bosnia and Herzegovina. My town was a small town with a town square, and around the town were farms, fields, and forest.

My childhood was happy. I lived with no fear. I had the freedom to go wherever I wanted to go. I could spend my time in town or ride my bike to my grandmother's farm and help her with the cows. I could play in the forest with my friends.

On a normal day, before the war, I would get up and go to school. I would walk home after school, or maybe walk to my grandparents' house, or ride my bike to my grandmother's farm. My father worked in construction, and my mother worked in a clothing factory making T-shirts and things like that, so my little brother and I spent a lot of time with my grandparents. My father's parents lived near us, and my mother's parents had a farm very near our town. My grandfather taught me to ride a bike and carve wood. He made me a little bow and arrows. We picked plums together. It was a good childhood.

I was in second grade when the war started. Then everything changed. One day a convoy of Serb Army trucks rolled into town. My mother told me to be quiet and look down. I was playing outside with a toy gun. I was so frightened that I took my little ax and chopped it up. We lived with fear.

Our home was next to the mosque. We were afraid that the Serbs would blow up the mosque and it would collapse on our house, so we moved from house to house looking for a safe place to sleep.

The whole town had a curfew. Everyone needed to be inside with the lights out by 10 p.m. Anyone outside after 10 p.m. might be shot. One of my uncles was shot coming home after curfew. My grandfather found his body the next morning. Another uncle was killed when a grenade was thrown into his house.

My father's friends were Serbian. They told him we needed to go away to stay safe. We were waiting for the money and the opportunity to leave. A convoy of buses was sent to get Muslims out of town. The Serbs called a twenty-four-hour ceasefire for us to leave, or else. My father's parents stayed behind because my grandmother's health was not good, but everyone else got on a bus and left. Now we were refugees in our own country. The buses took us to Travnik. We lived with about twenty-five or thirty other people in a gym locker room for three months. They shaved the men's heads—to prevent lice, they said.

Then we moved to Croatia. My mother's father gave us money to rent a house in Croatia. I went to school while we waited for the paperwork to go to Germany. Aunts, uncles, and cousins were all traveling to different places to find safety. We were all trying to find our way in the dark. We did not know where to go or how to get there. We did not know where the rest of our family and friends were until someone would get a call: "Your sister is here." "Uncle is there." The family that used to live all together ended up spread to all over the world.

After a year in Croatia, we moved to Germany. My mother's father had lived and worked in Germany as a guest worker after World War II, and he was able to sponsor us. We were really just following blindly; we did not know where to go. We did not know how to be refugees, how to get help, or where we would be safe. Germany allowed us to stay until the war was over, but the German government said that when the war was over, we must go back to Bosnia. We got a lawyer to help us stay in Germany longer. We did not want to go back.

I went to school in Germany. In school in Bosnia, I was required to learn the Cyrillic alphabet (the alphabet used for Russian) and the Latin alphabet (the alphabet used for English and German), so I knew the alphabet. I learned German and studied in school. We lived in Germany for six years.

At the beginning of the war, one of my mother's cousins had gone straight to the USA. He was able to sponsor us to come to the USA for family reunification in 1998. The UNHCR and Catholic Refugee Services helped us to move to the USA.

Everything I knew about the USA I learned from 1990s TV and movies in Germany; we didn't have TV in Bosnia. All I knew was from Hollywood. I was in for a huge culture shock.

I was fifteen when I arrived in Spokane. After Germany, Spokane seemed like a small town. There was so much open land and nothingness. Then school started. I looked different, I had the wrong clothes and the wrong haircut, and I didn't speak the language, but I had been through this before. Everything clicked in: "This was where I am now." I had been exposed to new cultures and languages before; I had adjusted to all this before.

In Spokane I took English as a Second Language classes with students from other countries. For the first six months, I felt and looked like I did not belong. My only friends were ESL students. It took a while to fit in. I was just finishing seventh grade when I left Germany, but in Spokane I was put in tenth grade because of my age, so I never had eighth or ninth grade. School was confusing. There were so many choices. In Germany there were no individual choices; we were told what classes to take. In the USA it was all about individual choices: "What do you want to do? What do you want to become?" I had a voice I didn't know how to use. It was hard to handle. Fortunately, other students took me under their wing and helped me.

I took a city bus to school. I made friends there too because I knew the music teenagers were listening to. I was the first Bosnian student to take driver's ed and get a license. My parents bought me a car so that I could take them to appointments and translate for them and the rest of the Bosnian community in Spokane. Sometimes I felt like a child with no voice of my own. I had to do what my parents told me. I was always translating for someone. Parents were struggling too—I could see it in their eyes—and I had to do what needed to be done. It was humbling, and it made me feel old sometimes.

Getting a driver's license at sixteen (in Germany the driving age is eighteen) was great. Having a car allowed me to venture out and meet people. I didn't have to stay home anymore. I could drive anywhere. My friends and I would drive around Spokane listening to music and talking.

As my English improved, I took more mainstream classes. I took German class, where I was able to help American students, which felt good. I had teachers who recognized the trauma and agony I had been through, but they helped me focus. They saw potential in me and encouraged me. I learned computer and technology skills and language skills. I managed to have good grades too. After three years in high school, I was ready to graduate.

## Epilogue

When I graduated from high school, my counselor said, "A four-year university isn't the right first step for you. You should start at the community college." So I started at Spokane Falls Community College. There I made friends who were transferring to Washington State University (WSU) in Pullman, Washington. They told me I should go with them. Figuring out how to do the college application and scholarship paperwork was hard, but I was able to go to WSU and graduated with a degree in psychology and German.

I thought maybe I would become a therapist, but I couldn't afford to go to graduate school right away. I got a job at Nordstrom's and started to work my way into management.

In 2013, I was diagnosed with cancer. While I was going through chemotherapy and working at the same time, I decided I needed to do something else. I moved into Nordstrom's corporate offices in Seattle, using computer skills I had started to develop in high school. I joined a training team to create training materials to help people learn how to look at statistics and do analysis. I became a teacher.

After I finished my cancer treatment, I was told there was a very small chance that the cancer would return. In 2014, I was diagnosed with cancer again, and again I kept working through my treatment.

After years with Nordstrom's, I changed jobs to work for F5 Networks [a technology company], working with network engineers. My people skills, developed by moving through many countries and cultures and years of working in sales at Nordstrom's, helped me get this job.

I am now cancer free. I continue looking for ways to live a better, healthier life. I do yoga and eat right and try to live a healthy life. I have gone to counseling for PTSD, and it is helpful to be able to talk about feelings and experiences. I am still here, and I have gone beyond just surviving, I am living a good life.

My family is doing well in the USA. My little brother went to the University of Washington and Georgetown University and studied political science and international relationships analysis. He works in Washington, DC.

The USA is our home now. I lived in Bosnia for eight years, in Croatia for one year, and in Germany for six years; the rest of my life has been here in the USA. This is home.

I would like Americans to understand that refugees and immigrants are just like anyone else. It is difficult to say, "Put yourself in their shoes," because you can't. There has not been a war here in this country for over a hundred years, and I hope there never is a war here. If you have not been in a war, you cannot imagine it. But try to understand; give the refugee a chance. Share your love, your hope, and a little of what you have. Donate. Volunteer. Help each other. Be a better human. Talk to people who are different.

War does terrible things to people, but good can come from it too. People coming to America expose us to so much diversity, and that makes us, America, better.

# Mirza

Bosnia and Herzegovina
US Entry: 1999

My family and I were all born and raised in the city of Bijeljina, Bosnia and Herzegovina, which used to be Yugoslavia. My life in Bosnia was good. Every summer we went camping and enjoyed visits with family. Family is very important. My father built our house next to my grandparents' home, on the same lot. I have good memories of going to school, adventuring through my city, and visiting my first video arcade.

I would wake up in the morning, get ready, and walk to school. On my way, I would meet up with some kids from the neighborhood. We would visit the bakery on our way to school and buy treats with the money my mother gave me. After school I would play outside until dark.

When my grandfather received his pension each month, he would give me some money, and I would use it to go to the arcade and play games until I ran out of money. I went to school, I had lots of friends, we went on vacations. I had a very good childhood, until the war started.

I remember the fear when the war started. I remember nights filled with the explosions of bombs and the sounds of gunfire. I remember hiding in my wealthy neighbor's basement for days while the paramilitary Serb army was going through the city butchering Muslim people after robbing them. I remember my father going out, for days, thinking he would never come back. I remember fig jam on stale bread. I remember being hungry. I remember fleeing.

The war started suddenly, in the night. It was terrifying. We cheered when the military rolled into our town; we thought they were our liberators, the old Yugoslavian Army coming to protect us, until the killing started. My father's friend was killed by a sniper while we were welcoming this army. Without the Muslim community knowing it, our Orthodox Christian Serb neighbors had planned this war to wipe out the Muslims. We were so confused. Neighbors were turning on neighbors.

Fresh food became impossible to find. The local butcher was killed, so we had no fresh meat. The local baker was killed, so we had no fresh bread. There was no food in the shops.

I left Bosnia in March 1992, when I was six years old. I had just learned to ride a bike. I had snuck into the attic and discovered a brand-new red BMX bike hidden there that was going to be my birthday present that summer. I had to leave it there without ever riding it. My grandmother, my father's mother, insisted that we leave. My father did not want to leave his home, but his mother convinced him to take the family and leave. She wanted us to survive, but she stayed behind.

We had to pay someone a lot of money and leave in the middle of the night. My parents and I drove to another city, one that hadn't seen the war yet—Brčko, where one of my dad's sisters lived. From there, we rode a crowded bus to Germany.

The trip was frightening. We were stopped at the boarder by the paramilitary troops. They took several people off the bus, and those people did not make it back to the bus. Most likely they were killed. My mother told me to pretend I was asleep. I closed my eyes and pretended to sleep.

After twelve hours, we arrived in Nuremberg, Germany: tired, hungry, and frightened. Germany was so beautiful, with big buildings and bright lights. It was nothing like our small town. We got off the bus and into a Mercedes taxi that took us to another aunt's two-bedroom apartment. That apartment became the refugee center for our entire family of sixteen for the next three months, until we could find our own places. Aunts, uncles, and cousins came from different places in Bosnia and gathered together in Nuremburg. My family found an apartment to share with another family. After a year, we were able to get our own apartment. I went to school there and learned German. I was in a class to help me transition into German school. I picked up German pretty easily. We the spent seven years in Germany.

We submitted our paperwork to come to the USA in 1995. Three years later, in 1998, we received the letter telling us to come for our interviews and medical checkups.

We had to travel three hours to Frankfurt to have the interviews. We were very stressed; there was no guarantee that we would be accepted to go to America. Right before our turn to go in front of the judge for our interview, a man came out crying. He had been denied. My mother told me, "Tell the judge you are afraid to go back. There is nothing there for us." Which was true. There was nothing for us to go back to. Our home and everything we had was gone.

We went in front of the judge and told her our story. The judge said we were accepted. My mother cried. Then we had very thorough physical exams. Nine months later we had our tickets to go to America. The USA bought the tickets for us, and then we had to pay the government back for everything they had given us to get started.

We flew from Frankfurt to Chicago to Spokane. In the airport in Chicago I ate at McDonald's, and I didn't know how to order. I didn't know how to say fries; I said, "Pommes frites"—*fried potatoes* in German—and I just pointed. I got a Big Mac and fries. It was good.

Everything I knew about America came from 1990s movies. I was relieved when I found that schools here in America were nothing like the schools in movies. Still, I was very worried about learning to speak English and fitting in.

Our arrival went smoothly. My grandmother, aunt, and uncle had arrived in Spokane before us. The night we arrived in Spokane, they brought a big group of fellow Bosnian refugees to welcome us. They showed us the way. The first morning I woke up in Spokane was a quiet, peaceful summer day. It was wonderful.

We spent our first days in my aunt and uncle's beautiful apartment, and I hoped we could find an apartment nearby. We found an apartment very quickly, but it was not nearly as nice. I cannot remember problems during our first days in America, but I do recall problems on the first day of school.

The first day, in gym class, we were playing basketball. A ball bounced off me and hit another boy. He came at me and called me, "F***ing Russian!" I hated being called a Russian. I head-butted him. The teacher was nice about it, but he had to send me to the office. The principal was nice to me too, but he had to help me understand that fighting was not acceptable. People at school were good to me. I learned English. I made friends. I got a job. I went to the skills center and learned computer technology.

Coming to America was a new beginning.

## Epilogue

Being a teenager, listening to hip-hop, in America in the 1990s, was as cool as it could get. It was exciting. At the same time, it was boring because in Spokane, Washington the public transportation is very limited. To go any place or do anything,

I needed a car to get around, and I did not have a car. There wasn't any place for young people to go to listen to music and dance. After Germany, this was really hard to get used to.

Some things in America were confusing. The prices in stores do not include the tax. Tax is not added until you check out. It does not make sense.

I am a business analyst. I have been working for the same company for sixteen years and have moved up the corporate ladder. I like my job. I am married with two stepchildren. I own my home. My parents live next door. My dream now is to live comfortably with my family and have my health when I retire.

Every person just wants what is best for their family. Every person has the right to the pursuit of happiness and prosperity for themselves and their family. Borders are decided by the lucky winners, and while one person may be born in a place that has no running water and another is born into a stable, middle-class family in Washington, neither one chose where they would be born.

I would not be here if my family was not forced to leave, but in retrospect, I am happy we came here.

# Shaban

**Kosovo**
**US Entry: 1999**

O nce upon a time, long ago on February, 1983, I was born in Ferizay, Kosovo. I was a little boy in Kosovo.

When I was growing, I was a very happy child. I had a nice family: Mother, Father, older brothers Jeton and Arben, me, and my little sister Teuta. My family was very happy.

I left my country because a war started and would kill everybody who stayed at home.

The day I left my country was March 15, 1999. I was sixteen years old. I will never forget that day I said to my house, "Bye, bye."

Then we drove on a tractor to the border, but bad people said, "You are not going to go!"

I stayed there on the border with my family for twenty-four hours. We did not have anything to eat.

The next day, in the morning, we went back to another city, and my family stayed with a family we had never met before. We were strangers, but they let us stay and gave us food. My brother, my dad, and I stayed only two days.

After two days, my brother, my dad, and I had to leave. There were people who wanted to kill all Muslim men. We had no way to go, but we needed to cross the big mountains into Macedonia. My mom was very sad because she and my sister could not come; it was too far and too dangerous.

We walked through the mountains for two days and one night. We walked through the night. In the morning when

I saw where we had walked, I saw it was very dangerous and scary. The cliffs were very high and full of snow.

After we got to Macedonia, the bad police took us. They said, "Why do you come to Macedonia? You are terrorists! We need to kill you!"

A policeman took a big knife and said, "I'm going to kill you because you are terrorists!" Then the police put my brother and me in one small room and my father in another room. They beat us. They asked us questions, but we did not speak their language, so we could not answer. They asked for money, but we did not have any money.

After police finished beating my brother and me, he put my brother, my dad, and me in a car and they told us the driver would take us to the border and the Serbian people would kill us.

Instead, the police took us to a big refugee camp in Macedonia. I stayed for sixteen days. In this camp, I worked to help people. I handed out blankets, drink, and food. Every day, I looked for my mother and my sister. I saw people coming and coming, but not my mother and sister. I was very sad.

After sixteen days of staying in the camp, my dad, my brother, and I found transportation to my cousin in the Skopje, and there I saw my grandpa.

For two weeks we stayed in Skopje [Macedonia]. Then my mom called from another refugee camp and said, "Come and get us. We are in Macedonia."

When my mom and my sister were with us, we went back to my cousin's house. Everybody was happy because my sister and mom were still alive. We were all together, and we were alive.

We could not stay with my cousin. The house was too small. We did not have money for food, and we feared the war would be coming there too.

After one week, my family and I went to another refugee camp. My family and I wanted to go to another country to live and earn money because in my country we couldn't live, and in Macedonia we didn't have enough money.

After one month in the camp, the papers came to our tent. The papers told my family that everything was ready and after two days we would start to go to the United States.

Then I, with my family, started our journey to the United States. We traveled from Macedonia to Athens, then to New York, then to Chicago, and from Chicago to Spokane by plane.

I went to Ferris High School. I learned English and many other important subjects during the day and got a job working at a restaurant at night. I began a new life in America, but I never forgot my country.

## Epilogue

I graduated from high school and went to college, where I studied nursing. My sister graduated and went to university and became a dentist. My family is happy in the United States, happy to live and work in peace. I am married now. My wife and I have beautiful children who have never known war. Life is good.

NORTH AMERICA

ATLANTIC
OCEAN

AFRICA

PACIFIC
OCEAN

SOUTH
AMERICA

E

# PART 4

# THE AMERICAS

In 1507 German mapmaker Martin Waldseemuller made a map of the American continents and labeled them America in honor of the Italian explorer Amerigo Vespucci. The Americas includes two continents, North America and South America. North America includes the land north of the Panama-Colombia border, and South America is the land below it. There are two distinct cultural groups in the Americas. Latin America includes all the countries south of the Rio Grande at the border of the United States, and Mexico, including all of South America and the West Indies. Anglo-America includes all of Canada and the United States.

AREA: North America—9.54 million square miles (24.7 million sq. km)
South America—6.89 million square miles (17.8 million sq. km)

POPULATION: North America—579 million
South America—423.58 million

COUNTRIES: North America—twenty-three
South America—fourteen

LANGUAGES: North America—English, Spanish, French, and hundreds of other languages
South America—Spanish, Portuguese, and several other languages

RELIGIONS: North America—Christianity, Judaism, Buddhism, Islam, Agnosticism/Atheism, and many Indigenous religions and other religions
South America—Christianity, Judaism, Buddhism, Islam, Hinduism, Bahá'í Faith, Shintoism, and several other religions

*ATLANTIC OCEAN*

*Mexico*

*PACIFIC OCEAN*

**SOUTH AMERICA**

AMERICA

CHAPTER 17

# MEXICO

• • • • • • • • • • • • • • • • • • • • • • • • • • • • • • • • • • • • • • • • • • • • • •

## A Few Facts about Mexico

**AREA:** 758,450 square miles (1,964,375 sq. km)

**POPULATION:** 126.42 million

**LANGUAGES:** Spanish and Indigenous languages

**RELIGIONS:** Christianity and traditional religions

## A Little History

Many different Indigenous people lived in what we now call Mexico long before Europeans arrived in the early 1500s. The Olmec, Mayan, and Aztec cultures built large cities and had complex societies. Although they were very advanced civilizations, they were unable to defeat the Spanish conquistadors who colonized Mexico. About 90 percent of Indigenous

Americans died from European diseases and the harsh treatment of the Spanish.

Over time, the people of the Spanish colony divided into two groups: "pure Spanish" Criollos and Mestizos of mixed Spanish and Indigenous descent. The Criollos were the rich and powerful, and the Mestizos were the laborers.

In 1821 Mexico won independence from Spain. At the time of independence, Mexico was much larger than it is today. Texas declared independence from Mexico in 1836 and later joined the United States. Between 1846 and 1848, Mexico and the United States fought the Mexican-American War. At the end of that war, Mexico ceded what is now California, Nevada, Utah, Arizona, and New Mexico to the United States, reducing the size of Mexico by one-third. After the Mexican-American War, the government introduced many reforms and wrote a new constitution, which guaranteed many civil rights. But the new constitution reduced the power of the Catholic Church, and this led to civil war, which weakened the country. In 1861 Mexico came under the control of France but regained independence in 1867.

The new government encouraged foreign investment, and by 1910 most of the large businesses in Mexico were owned by foreigners, mostly British or American. Modernization and economic growth benefited wealthy Mexicans and businesspeople from other countries, not the majority of Mexicans, who remained poor. The inequality and lack of opportunity led to years of civil war. In 1923 the United States recognized the government of Mexico on the condition that their leaders promised not to take over the American oil companies in Mexico. With the discovery of oil, Mexico experienced industrial and economic growth that caused the wealth gap between the rich and the poor to grow. In the 1970s, the Mexican government promised to improve social welfare and borrowed money to fund it, leaving the country with a huge national debt. The continued wealth gap has caused internal conflict. Many Mexican people live in poverty and have few job opportunities. Since the 1980s, drug cartels moving drugs through Mexico to markets in the United States have instigated kidnappings, killings, and intimidation campaigns that endanger Mexicans.

## Why Do People Leave?

Because job opportunities in many parts of Mexico are scarce, many Mexicans come to the United States to work and send money back to their families. People also flee drug-related violence.

# Estella

**Mexico**
**US Entry: 1984, 1990**

I was born in the small village of Tilalchapa in the Guerrero State of Mexico. I am the youngest in my family, I have an older sister and three older brothers. We had a simple, happy life, surrounded by aunts and uncles, cousins, and grandparents.

When I was young, we would run by the river chasing butterflies. We climbed mango trees and sat in the trees eating mangoes. On hot days we swam in the river. Little children do not understand what it means to be rich or poor. We had what we had, and we were happy.

When I was very small, my father went north to the United States to work. After a few years, my mother decided to join my father in California. She took me with her. My brothers and sister stayed with our abuela [grandmother] in Guerrero.

The bus trip to America was long, hot, and scary. Mother packed food to eat along the way. Everything was new and different. The bus made many stops. Finally, after days of travel, we came to Tijuana, where my mother had friends we could stay with. I didn't really understand what we were doing, and I was a little afraid.

My mother woke me up at 2 a.m. Two very young men, "coyotes," were there to take us across the border. We walked quietly in the dark. I could hear dogs barking in the distance.

"Hurry, hurry," the coyotes whispered. We crossed a fence, and a car was waiting for us. My mother sat in the back of the car with a blanket over her lap, and I hid behind her legs.

The next day, I met my father. I didn't remember him. I was too little when he left.

We arrived in the spring, almost the end of the school year, but I started school in second grade. A very nice teacher came to help me learn English at the back of the classroom. It seemed like I learned English very fast. The next year I went to third grade.

My parents arranged for my brothers to come to join us in California, but my sister stayed with our grandmother in Mexico.

When I was in fourth grade, my parents were working in the fields. One day, Immigration came to the fields where they were working. My mother ran, but my father was not fast enough. My father was caught and got deported. Now my mother had to support us by herself.

My father decided to come back to the United States. With a cousin, he came back to the border. They had to swim across a canal. The cousin swam in front, and my father followed. Something happened—maybe he got a cramp or something. My father went under the water and did not come back up. It was dark. Our cousin looked for him, but he could not find him.

A few days later, we were told that some bodies were found in the canal. One of them was my father. A friend had to go and identify the body. A little girl had drowned there too, but no one knew whose little girl she was. The bodies of the people they found were buried together in El Centro [California], with numbers to mark their grave.

As poor as everyone was, they still collected money to help us. My mother decided to take me back to Mexico. My brothers stayed in California with cousins. My oldest brother felt like he needed to be the man of the family now and earn money to take care of us.

I went to fifth and sixth grade in Mexico. We lived with Abuela and took care of her for two years, but then she passed away. My mother decided to go back to the United States. This time my sister came with us.

In Tijuana, the police kidnapped us and held us for ransom. They said, "Give us money and we will let you go." Somehow, we got away and ran. We crossed through the desert.

In California, a friend of my mother's married her and adopted us girls. Now we were legal residents of the United States. My mother was able to get legal immigration papers and a green card too. Finally, we were safe in America.

In 1990 we moved to Spokane. When I started in school again, I remembered how to speak English. My sister started to learn English. We went to school together and started to think about what we would do in life.

## Epilogue

I graduated from high school in 1996 and started to go to community college. I got a job working in medical billing. My mother had medical problems, and the medicals bills started to get very high. My sister and I worked to help pay our mother's medical bills. Later I started working for an insurance company. My sister and I became certified medical interpreters. Sometimes when I help a family, I see children helping their parents interpret and I think, "That was me," since I was a child I helped to interpret for my mother, read documents for her,

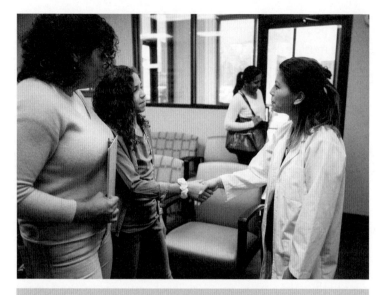

Medical interpreters are people who help translate information from doctors to their patients.

and helped her pay the bills. When I interpret, I feel like I am making a difference in someone's life. I want to help people and have a positive impact on others.

Now I am married with two daughters. My daughters work hard in school. One wants to be a doctor someday. I feel so lucky to be here in the United States. Life in the United States has been worth risking our lives to get here. Our dad died to give us a better life. I teach my children to never take anything for granted, to be good, to share, to help others, and to appreciate everything you have.

# Ivan

**Mexico**
**US Entry: 2007**

My mother and father are from Casa Grande, Mexico. Casa Grande is a small town in the Mexican state of Chihuahua, near the border with the state of New Mexico in the United States.

When I was small, two or three years old, my family moved to the capital city of Chihuahua. In Chihuahua I had a good life. My family was a happy family. My younger brothers and I would wake up in the morning, and our father would take us to school on his way to work. He would pick us up and take us home for lunch each day. Our family was together, and in our culture that is the most important thing. After school, we would do our homework and then play soccer or ride bikes with our friends. Life was good.

We had tourist visas to visit the United States, and we took many vacations in the United States. We visited friends and family in Arizona and California. My grandmother lived in Mesa, Arizona.

When I was a little older, the drug cartels started to move into our city. The president of Mexico, Filipe Calderon, had declared a war on drugs, but the drug cartels were not giving up easily. They started extorting money from businesses. My father had a business rebuilding automobile parts. The drug cartel sent people to talk to him. They wanted to know how much money he was making with his business.

He asked, "Why do you need to know how much money I earn?"

"You will pay us a percentage of what you earn," they told him. "If you do not pay us, we will ruin your business."

My father did not want to pay these drug cartels. He would not let him extort money from him or ruin his business. My father talked to my mother, and they agreed they would rather close their business than do business with the drug cartels. My father had a cousin who lived and worked in Spokane, Washington, in the United States. His cousin needed to hire workers to help him in his job. My father decided he would go north to work with his cousin.

When my father went north, I had to become the man of the family and help to feed my family. My mother got a job and told me I needed to focus on school, but on weekends I worked, any kind of job I could get, to help feed the family.

A year later, right after my fifteenth birthday, we traveled north too. First, we drove to Arizona to visit my grandmother. We spent a couple of months with her. I had been to Arizona many times before, so I was comfortable in the United States. I was used to hearing people speak English. In school, I had started to study English in middle school. Still, I had a lot of worries and "what ifs." If we moved to Spokane with my father, how would we survive? We did not have a lot of friends and family in Spokane. There would be no one to help us if we needed help.

In September, right after Mexican Independence Day, we flew to Spokane. Until then, every place I had visited in the USA had looked a lot like Chihuahua, Mexico. Arizona was hot, dry desert, just like Chihuahua. Spokane was a different world! The city of Spokane was about the same size as the city of Chihuahua, but everything else was different. There were snowy mountains, lakes, rivers, and green forests. Everything was a lot greener.

My mother got a job working with my father in a hotel. My brothers and I went to school. The schools were different. In Mexico we wore uniforms, but in Spokane students could wear whatever they wanted. I had studied physics and calculus in middle school, but in the United States these classes are not taught until high school. Of course, the biggest difference was that everything was taught in English. I took English as a Second Language classes and met people from all over the world. My classmates came from many different countries: Russia, the Marshall Islands, Burma, Sudan, Ethiopia, Burundi, and Haiti—and one other student was from Mexico. The only things we had in common were learning English and soccer. Soccer brought us all together.

I was a good student in Mexico. Even though I'd studied math in Mexico, it was the hardest class for me in high school. The math procedures used in America are different. We get the same answers, but we take a different path. There was a language barrier. Without good English skills, it was hard to explain the procedures. Learning English was a big priority.

Our family lifestyle changed in Spokane. My brothers and I spent six or seven hours each day at school, just like in Mexico, but now I ate lunch at school. After school I still did my homework, but in America young people do not play soccer and ride bikes after school; they play a lot of video games and do things inside instead of outside. It was hard to get used to staying inside. I have always been talkative, and that helped me make friends. My parents always taught me to hold my head up. They said, "Never let anyone talk you down, be proud of who you are, and always be honest and fair." I have never felt like I do not belong. I am accepted by the other students and my teachers too.

The most confusing thing about Spokane was the weather. Spokane can have four seasons in one day! I learned to live with the crazy weather and even enjoy the snow. One of my mother's friends took us to the mountains, and I learned to snowboard. Snowboarding was the most fun!

My junior year, I started to take classes at the Spokane Skills Center to learn auto mechanics and prepare for my future career. I'd always liked to work with my hands, to fix things and build things. If we had stayed in Mexico, I would have been part of my father's business repairing auto parts. In the United States, I want to be a mechanic and have my own automotive shop someday. America is a land of opportunity for anyone who is willing to work hard.

## Epilogue

After graduating from high school, I wanted to go to the auto mechanic program at the community college, but there was no money for school. I had come to the United States with a tourist visa; I did not have the right papers to get financial aid for college. My parents and I did not have enough money to pay for college.

I got a job working in a hotel and worked hard. I met and dated a wonderful woman. When our relationship started to get serious, I told her that I did not have the right papers to live and work in the United States. I wanted to be honest with her, and I did not want her to think that I wanted to marry her to improve my immigration status. She was understanding, and we got married. When we were expecting our first child, she came to me and said it was time to fix my immigration papers. I worked with an immigration lawyer to get the right papers to live and work in the United States. I did not want to risk being deported and missing my child growing up. There was a lot of paperwork, and it was very expensive, but I am glad that I was able to do that.

I was very successful in my job at the hotel and became a general manager by the time I was twenty-two, but I did not like the lifestyle. There were too many hours and too much stress. I was married and had a child, but in this job, I did not have time for my family. My family is everything to me. I needed to spend time with them.

I talked it over with my wife and decided to change careers. I had always liked working with my hands, so I found a new job with a friend who worked in the roofing business. It was hard work, but I learned fast. I decided to start my own roofing business. I am proud to be able to do clean, quality work and see my customer's appreciation when I do a good job.

Sometimes, I meet people who are racist and say things that are very rude. I meet them with polite manners and hard work. For example, once I had a job roofing a house for a man who did not like Mexicans. He greeted us with very derogatory words. I could have been rude back to him, but I met him with, "Good morning, sir." He was surprised that I could speak English. We roofed his house and left his yard cleaner than when we started. We changed his mind about Mexicans. He apologized for being rude to us. I want to change people's minds.

People need to understand that immigrants are not the enemy. We are just trying to live our lives and provide for our families. No one wants to allow their family to suffer or go hungry; we do what we have to do to take care of our families. We are just humans with needs. We all make choices, and then we have to live them. I am here now, and I have to work and make my dreams come true. I want my son to do what he wants to do, to achieve his dreams. I will support him 100 percent. That is the American Dream.

NORTH AMERICA

ATLANTIC OCEAN

Guatemala
El Salvador

SOUTH
AMERICA

CHAPTER 18

# EL SALVADOR AND GUATEMALA

## A Few Facts about El Salvador

**AREA:** 8,124 square miles (21,040 sq. km)

**POPULATION:** 6.49 million

**LANGUAGES:** Spanish and Indigenous languages

**RELIGIONS:** Christianity

# A Few Facts about Guatemala

**AREA:** 42,043 square miles (108,889 sq. km)

**POPULATION:** 15.43 million

**LANGUAGES:** Spanish and Indigenous languages

**RELIGIONS:** Christianity and Mayan

# A Little History

The original people of El Salvador and Guatemala had complex societies, built pyramids, and created large cities. Some of those cities are still inhabited.

After the Spanish arrived in Central America in 1524, Indigenous people resisted Spain's attempts to colonize their land. But the Spanish had better weapons and brought European diseases that killed many people. The Spanish established the colony of Guatemala, with El Salvador as one of its provinces. El Salvador was the agricultural center of the Guatemalan colony. The Indigenous people were forced to farm and work the land for the Spanish.

Many areas in Central America declared independence in the early 1800s. Guatemala, El Salvador, Honduras, Nicaragua, and Costa Rica united to form the Federal Republic of Central America in 1823. These countries fought over how their government would be run until the republic broke apart into independent countries in 1841.

The newly independent countries continued to have internal disagreements and international conflicts. When coffee became an important commercial crop, the economies and governments of Central America became stronger, but the people lacked basic human rights. Governments sold Indigenous people's land to wealthy coffee growers. When people rebelled, governments used the military to silence them. Soon the coffee industry was controlled by just a few wealthy families. With very little land of their own, most Indigenous people could not raise enough food to support themselves, so they were forced to work for the big coffee plantations for very low wages.

Many US companies built factories in Central American countries to take advantage of the low wages. The US government provided aid to the governments to help keep these companies successful.

In the 1970s, rebels organized to overthrow their governments. The more people protested, the more the governments cracked down on human rights. Suspected rebels were arrested and never seen again. Death squads targeted religious leaders, students, teachers, and anyone who spoke against the government.

## Why Do People Leave?

Government death squads forced many Salvadorans and Guatemalans to flee for their lives in the 1980s. More recently, people have left to escape the threats of gang violence and drug cartels. Often, people must choose between joining or helping a gang or being killed. Some try a third option: undertaking the dangerous journey to the United States, where they can apply for asylum—which the US government rarely grants—or enter the country without documentation and risk deportation if their status is discovered.

# Luisa

**El Salvador**
**US Entry: 1983**

I was born in El Salvador. El Salvador is a beautiful, warm, green country, with flowers blooming at all times of the year. My family did not have a lot of money, but we were rich in other ways; we had each other and our faith. With many brothers and sisters, cousins, aunts, and uncles, I was never lonely. Our life was simple but good. I lived in a village that did not have electricity or running water. I remember laughing and running up and down a steep hill with my cousins while carrying heavy buckets of water on our heads. From the beginning of my life I was surrounded by love, laughter, and prayer.

My parents were good parents, helping us to grow up recognizing the difference between good and bad, right and wrong. Once, one of my older brothers was working in a field a long way from the house, and my mother asked me and one of my younger brothers to take him some lunch to eat. The way was long and hot. We took him his lunch and then started home. Along the way we had to pass a field of watermelon. The watermelons looked so good, so ripe. My little brother and I could imagine how good a watermelon would taste on a hot day like that. The field was full of watermelons.

One of us said, "It would be so good to eat one of those watermelons."

The other said, "Maybe the farmer would not miss one watermelon."

We knew it was wrong, but we took one watermelon and

went down to the river and ate that watermelon. It was so good, so refreshing and sweet. We washed in the river and went on home, contented with our bellies full of watermelon.

When we arrived home, my father asked us, "How was your walk? Did you give your brother his lunch?" We told him that we had. Then he asked, "Did you do anything else?"

We told him, "No, we just gave him his lunch and came back home."

"Are you sure you did not stop and eat our neighbor's watermelon?" he asked.

We tried to say, "No, we did not eat a watermelon," but we were not very convincing. We thought we had cleaned ourselves well, but we still had watermelon seeds sticking to our skin and in our hair. My father picked a watermelon seed from my hair and showed it to me. "Are you sure?" he asked.

My father had us take each seed still stuck to us and plant it. We tended that watermelon patch until the watermelons were ripe, and then we gave all the watermelons to our neighbor to atone for our theft. That was the kind of man our father was. He did not beat us, he did not scream at us. He showed us what was right and wrong and helped us make amends.

My parents believed that the Gospel must be lived. They taught us that we cannot call ourselves Christian if we do not love and serve one another. They taught us to be honest and humble.

In the 1970s and 1980s, the government of El Salvador was a military dictatorship. Government policies were oppressive. People had no rights. The government used violence to control the people. People who disagreed with the government were arrested and tortured. Sometimes people who spoke out against the government were "disappeared." Soldiers would come for that person, and no one would ever see that person again.

My father was a deacon in the church and sometimes went to San Salvador to meet with Archbishop Oscar Romero. Archbishop Romero believed that Christians must defend the rights of the poor and spoke against the government violence. Like Archbishop Romero, my parents spoke out for social justice. This was very dangerous.

In March of 1980, Archbishop Romero was assassinated while celebrating Mass. My family knew that the death squads would be coming for my father soon.

My father preached and quoted Archbishop Romero: "If they kill me, I will be resurrected among my people and be a seed of hope." Someone reported him to the government.

My family left our village and spent two years evading the government death squads, but one night they found us. They took my father, and we never saw him again.

My mother knew that we had to leave El Salvador, so we started walking north to the United States. Sometimes we all walked, and sometimes the older children would carry the younger children. Sometimes we were very hungry and tired. Along the way we were helped by churches. My sisters and I would sing in the churches, and the priests would ask people to help us because we were fleeing El Salvador.

Sometimes we took a bus. Buses were dangerous because sometimes soldiers would stop them. I saw soldiers take people off a bus and shoot them. I prayed for the soldiers to stop the killing.

We crossed Guatemala; we traveled through Mexico. Every day and every night we prayed for God's protection. Our journey was filled with miracles. One night, we were sleeping in the doorway of a big building, and the security guard found us. He did not call the police, though. He took us to the home of a priest. The priest asked a woman to give us a ride in her car.

We drove for hours. Then the car just stopped. My mother told us all to get out and pray. We knelt around the car and prayed. Then we got back in the car, and it started. We were taken to another priest who connected us to the Sanctuary Movement in the United States.

We took a train north toward the US/Mexican border. When we stopped, we were met by members of the Sanctuary Movement. They drove us in a van to the border. People from the Sanctuary Movement would meet us on the other side of the border, but first we had to cross the border. It was a hot day, and the sun was beating down on us. We prayed and we ran. Suddenly rain was pouring down and we could hardly see. This meant the border patrol also could not see us. We made it across the border and found the people from Sanctuary and their van.

They drove us to a church, where we stayed for a while. We stopped in many places but finally we came to Spokane, Washington. In Spokane we lived in the basement of a church.

I was fourteen years old, and soon I enrolled in high school. I had to learn English and everything that American students learn. Sometimes I felt so stupid, because I did not understand English well enough to understand my school-work, but I kept working at it. I graduated from high school and started college.

## Epilogue

In 1989, the US government granted protection and work permits to the Central American people who had come to the United States to seek refuge.

I became a teacher, teaching English to students like me who came to the United States looking for freedom and peace.

I became a US citizen and got married. I continue to teach and to be active in the church and community.

In 2015, I traveled to El Salvador for Archbishop Romero's beatification [a step toward official sainthood in the Catholic Church]. Pope Francis recognized my father as a martyr of the Catholic Church. In 2018, my mother traveled to Italy for the canonization of Saint Romero.

Archbishop Óscar Romero (*pictured*) was canonized as a saint by Pope Francis on October 14, 2018.

# Cruz

**El Salvador**
**US Entry: 2016**

I was born in a small city in El Salvador. The land where I lived is rural. There are volcanic mountains with flat land and valleys between them. The weather is always warm, and everything is green there. There are fruit trees, like citrus and mango trees, and flowers everywhere. My country is very beautiful.

A normal day in my country was waking up at 4 or 5 a.m. to work in agriculture—most people work in agriculture there—or to get ready for school. School started at 7 a.m. At noon I would go home for lunch. We had one hour for lunch, then I would go back to school until 5 p.m. After school I would go home, do my homework, and play soccer with my friends.

On weekends, people would gather together to play soccer. The games were free. Everyone would come to cheer for their teams. Families would bring picnics and spend the afternoon together. Spending time together with family is very important in my culture, and everyone loves soccer.

My best memories are of going to high school. My high school was up the mountain above my city. The city was always very hot, but the school was cool and surrounded by pine trees. That is the only place I saw pine trees in my country.

My country is very beautiful, but my city was not a safe place for young people. The economy in my city was very bad; there were no jobs for the people. Even people who had gone to school could not find jobs. The gangs caused a lot of trouble for people. I could not go outside after 6 p.m. If young people are outside after 6 p.m., someone will get them—either the gangs or the police. If the police find someone outside after 6 p.m., there is nothing that person can say—they are going to jail.

My parents were divorced, and my father lived in the United States. My mother wrote to my father and asked him to help me go to America. He said he would help, but he was remarried and had a new family. His wife did not know about me. He did not want me to come to the United States.

I told my family that I would go to the United States. One of my uncles had been to the United States and had come back again. He told me not to go; he said I might die. He said my body would not be strong enough to make the trip. My family argued. They got angry. They did not want me to go. They said, "You will die along the way." They did not believe I could make it. They were worried about me going, but I wanted a future. I did not want to stay in my city worrying about the gangs.

My mother said, "Maybe it is better that you go. God will protect you."

After school got out in June of 2016, I packed my school backpack with clothes and all the dollars I had, and I started my journey to the United States. One of my cousins came with me. My plan was to cross the US border, find the immigration police, and ask for asylum. I hoped that my father or my cousins in the United States would help me.

Four of us started our journey by car. Of course, it was easy to travel inside my country. We drove and camped. We would sleep a few hours and then continue on our way. The weather was good, the traveling was not hard, the countryside was similar to the land around my own city. We crossed into Guatemala, and from Guatemala City we took a bus to the border with Mexico.

At the border we had to cross a river in a small boat. Then we needed to be very careful. The Mexican police would deport us back to our country. They would not be nice to us. We exchanged some dollars for pesos, then we started to travel in a closed van. There were no windows for anyone to see in or out. The van was very hot. It was hard to breathe. The people who helped us were good people. Helping people to cross the border and travel through Mexico was their business.

We traveled like this for two days. When we got to Mexico City, we found an express bus that would take us closer to the border with Texas. This bus was protected; it would make no stops along the way. The windows were covered so no one could see in or out. I traveled with twenty-five people, mostly strangers, on this bus. We would eat once or twice each day. Some people had a hard time physically; they felt sick from riding so far in the hot, dark bus.

After a long time on this bus, we stopped and changed to a car. The car was open—we could see out. We traveled through the mountains in the night, to the border. We had to cross a small river to get to the United States. We waited there, camping by the river, for three days until the people who were guiding us were ready to take us across. We could see the drones in the sky patrolling the border.

Finally, it was time to cross the river. We crossed in a small boat. We could see a tall wooden guard tower. We walked for about ten to fifteen minutes. Then cars were coming, surrounding us. There were about ten cars. It was kind of scary, but we did not run. These were immigration officers.

They asked us, "Where are you from?" We were honest.

We answered their questions. We did not try to run away. So they said, "If you follow the rules, you will be okay."

I told them, "I have a cousin here."

I stayed in detention for a day and a half. It was all concrete and very uncomfortable. Then I was taken to a home for young people like me who had come the United States by themselves. This home was so much better than the immigration detention center. We had a school, food, and bedrooms. We could not leave except to go to church on Sundays. If we had good behavior, we could go places.

Living here was okay. I made good friends. Most of us had the same story. Some, the immigration police did not stop at the border. They looked like they were Americans, white with light hair. They had to look for the immigration police to turn themselves in.

While I was in this place, my cousins did the paperwork so I could live with them. Finally, I was told that I could go to my cousins in Spokane, Washington. The immigration police told me I would be okay if I followed the rules. I wanted to go to school, and they said I could go to school. I was so happy I could not sleep.

I flew from Dallas to Seattle, and then my cousins came to get me. My mother had told me I had cousins in Washington State, but I had not seen them since I was very small. I was a little nervous.

My cousins had legal papers to live and work in the United States. My father did too, but he would not help me. My cousins gave me a place to live, and I registered for school. My cousins did not care about school; they wanted me to go to work. I did not have a permit to work, though, and I did not want to get in trouble with immigration. I helped around the house and did everything I could do to be helpful, but I wanted to go to school, and they did not understand this. They got mad at me for not getting a job and working. They knew places that would hire me without a work permit. They said I could make good money. I just wanted to go to school and follow the rules.

I needed to study English and earn my high school diploma so I could go to college and have a career. In El Salvador I had studied English, but I never really believed I would need it. In the United States I studied hard. I have fun in high school, learning and making new friends. School is different in the United States. In El Salvador the same people stay together in all the classes, all day every day. In the United States, students go to different classes. Here I have friends from many different countries.

There are many differences between life in El Salvador and Spokane. In El Salvador, people spend a lot of time outside. People gather together in the community, like watching soccer games on weekend afternoons. People socialize outside of their homes. In America, people go to work and go home. They hardly ever go outside. This is very different from El Salvador.

School became my family. The people at the school helped me find a new place to live, with a family who understood that I needed to go to school. I moved, but I tried to stay connected to my cousins. They called my mother and told her I was a really bad kid. I told her I only want to go to school and stay out of trouble.

## Epilogue

I am working with an immigration lawyer now, and I am able to stay because I am still a student. In the future I hope that I will be able to get legal status. El Salvador is a different world, and I do not want to go back. I do not want to worry about gangs and violence. I hope to study computer science, and I want to help other people. I want to return the help I received. The United States has opportunity for anyone who is willing to work hard.

I want people to understand that immigrants just want to work, and we do the jobs that Americans do not want to do. We do not want to take something for nothing. We just want to create a better life for our families, for the next generation. We want to have the opportunity to make a better life.

# Anonymous

**Guatemala**
**US Entry: 2017**

O ne day in 2015 my grandfather said to me, "Nietecito [grandson], you need to go north to America." But I loved my life in Guatemala. I did not want to leave.

Another day he said to me again, "Nietecito, you must go to America."

But Guatemala is beautiful and warm. I had good friends. I was happy in Guatemala. I said, "No, I want to stay here."

And another day my grandfather and my grandmother came to me and said, "Nietecito, you need to leave. You must go to your mother in America."

My mother and my brother lived in Spokane, Washington. I lived with my grandparents. My grandparents wanted me to go to my mother to be safe.

Bad gangster people wanted to kill me. My grandparents knew that I had to go north or die.

I was scared because the Click 18 gang said, "We will come for you and your friends, we will kill you all."

The gangsters came to my school looking for me. I had to hide at school to avoid them.

Finally, I said, "Yes, I will go."

When I journeyed to America, I took the bus from my house to the center of Guatemala. I took another bus from Guatemala City to Mexico City. I spent a night in Mexico City. I slept in a hotel there and ate food in Mexico.

The next day I took a bus from Mexico City to Tijuana.

It was a long way. No one from my family was with me. I felt tired, sick, and lonely.

I spent a night in a hotel in Tijuana. I felt so lonely. The next day, I crossed into California and went to San Diego. I stay there ten days with cousins.

After ten days in San Diego, I came by airplane to Spokane, Washington. My mother met me at the airport. I like Spokane.

## Epilogue

Life in Spokane is much safer than life in Guatemala. I work. I help take care of my family. I stay away from trouble. I want to make a life for myself in the United States. I do not want to worry about gangs and drug dealers. I just want to live my life.

A Poem About Me
I am
Quiet, Dark, Friendly, Guatemalan,
Speaking Spanish, Speaking Kaqchikel,
Learning English,
Playing Soccer, Playing basketball
Listening to music
Loving family
Working hard
Dreaming of a good life
Me.

# CONCLUSION
# A New Home

Over twenty-six million people were refugees in 2020, according to the UNHCR. This number does not count asylum seekers or internally displaced people (people who have been forced to flee their homes yet remain in their countries). Half of these refugees are children. With only 1 percent of refugees being resettled each year, most refugees spend years in limbo, waiting for their lives to begin again.

People become refugees for many different reasons. War, political or religious persecution and gang- or drug-related violence are a few of the most common. Whatever the reasons, when refugees leave their homes, they do not just leave the violence and persecution; they also leave the life they know and the places they love. They often arrive in their new country with little more than memories and hope.

The United States is a land of immigrants and refugees. The United States is not immune to intolerance, and many newcomers have contended with anti-immigrant policies and attitudes, in addition to the hardships of learning a new language and adapting to a new culture. Still, people from around the world have relocated to the United States hoping to find more opportunities or freedoms than they experienced in their home countries. Throughout the country's history, immigrants and refugees have tackled the challenges of starting new lives in the United States. Some Americans believe that more immigrants than ever before are coming into the country. In fact, according to the US Census of 2020, 13.7 percent of the US population was born outside the United States—slightly less than in 1920, when 13.9 percent of the US population was born outside the United States. An overwhelming majority of people born in the United States are descendants of immigrants and refugees.

## What Can You Do If New Refugees Move in Next Door?

**Be a friend.** Stop by with food or a housewarming gift. Offer to drive your new neighbors somewhere that they need to go or to come along on an errand to keep them company. Tell them about yourself. Treat your new neighbor as an equal. Many of the people whose stories appear in this book remember and treasure the friendship and kindness of their new neighbors.

**Understand.** Moving from one country to another is hard even in the best of circumstances. Leaving family, friends, and everything familiar, knowing you cannot go back, is extremely painful. Do not assume that everyone is happy to be in the United States every day. Listen without judgment if your neighbors needs to vent, and only offer advice if they ask you for it.

**Share.** Teach some helpful English words, and learn some words in your neighbors' language. Help your neighbors learn about your community. Offer to introduce them to other people, make sure they know about local events and services, and volunteer to go with them to gatherings. Learn about the culture, the history, and the food of your neighbors' country.

**Encourage.** Adjusting to life in a new country is stressful and can be discouraging. Answer any questions your neighbors have. Celebrate whenever something positive happens in their life, whether it's getting a new job or moving to the next level of English class. At the same time, encourage your neighbors to continue to speak their language and hold on to the parts of their culture that they cherish.

# Source Notes

4     "What Is a Refugee?", USA for UNHCR, accessed April 1, 2021, https://www.unrefugees.org/refugee-facts/what-is-a-refugee/.

53    "Ethiopia, Eritrea Sign Joint Declaration of Peace," Voice of America, accessed April 16, 2021, https://www.voanews.com /africa/ethiopia-eritrea-sign-joint-declaration-peace.

# Further Reading

## Books

Brown, Don. *The Unwanted: Stories of the Syrian Refugees.* Boston: Houghton Mifflin Harcourt, 2018.
This graphic novel depicts the stories of hope and hardship of people affected by the Syrian refugee crisis.

Ellis, Deborah. *Children of War: Voices of Iraqi Refugees.* Toronto: Groundwood Books, 2009.
Read a collection of twenty stories of children living in refugee camps due to the Iraq War.

Gallo, Donald R., ed. *First Crossing: Stories about Teen Immigrants.* Cambridge, MA: Candlewick, 2009.
Eleven authors come together to share the stories of youth refugees relocating from political violence, war, and persecution.

Osbourne, Linda Barrett. *This Land Is Our Land: A History of American Immigration.* New York: Abrams, 2016.
Investigate the history of immigration in the United States and how past events influenced modern policy and attitudes.

Vecchione, Patrice, and Alyssa Raymond. *Ink Knows No Borders: Poems of the Immigrant and Refugee Experience.* New York: Triangle Square, 2019.
The poems of first- and second-generation immigrants and refugees depict how they navigate cultural and language barriers, handle stereotyping, and identity while maintaining hope.

Washington, John. *The Dispossessed: A Story of Asylum and the US-Mexican Border and Beyond.* New York: Verso, 2020.

The story of one man's quest to cross the border illuminates the historical, literary, and current political context to the discussion of migration today.

Yousafzai, Malala. *We Are Displaced.* New York: Little, Brown Books for Young Readers, 2019.

Part memoir, part communal storytelling, Nobel Peace Prize–winner Malala Yousafzai describes her journey out of Pakistan and explores the lives of girls she met along the way.

## Articles

5 of the Biggest Reasons Why People Become Refugees
https://www.globalcitizen.org/en/content/reasons-why-people-become-refugees/
Read about five different reasons people seek refuge.

## Organizations

International Organization for Migration (IOM)
https://www.iom.int/about-iom
The International Organization for Migration works with governments and other agencies to facilitate the migration of people between countries.

International Rescue Committee (IRC)
https://www.rescue.org/page/ircs-impact-glance
The International Rescue Committee is dedicated to helping people who are displaced by natural disasters or conflicts. They provide food, water, shelter, medical assistance, and education services to displaced people.

United Nations Children's Fund (UNICEF)
https://www.unicef.org/what-we-do
The United Nations Children's Fund is dedicated to providing children a safe and inclusive environment in which to grow. They provide resources for displaced children and children with disabilities.

United Nations High Commissioner for Refugees (UNHCR)
https://www.unhcr.org/en-us/about-us.html
The United Nations High Commissioner for Refugees helps refugees, displaced communities, and stateless people find asylum. They also work to protect their rights in their places of refuge.

World Relief
https://worldrelief.org/
World Relief is an organization that works with churches and volunteers to provide assistance to people suffering from natural disasters, poverty, oppression, violence, and displacement.

## Index